GARLAND STUDIES ON

INDUSTRIAL PRODUCTIVITY

edited by
STUART BRUCHEY
ALLAN NEVINS PROFESSOR EMERITUS
COLUMBIA UNIVERSITY

A GARLAND SERIES

MANAGEMENT STRATEGIES THAT MAKE U.S. FIRMS COMPETITIVE IN THE GLOBAL ECONOMY

TED REINGOLD

GARLAND PUBLISHING, Inc.
A MEMBER OF THE TAYLOR & FRANCIS GROUP
NEW YORK & LONDON / 1998

Library of Congress Cataloging-in-Publication Data

Reingold, Ted, 1948–
    Management strategies that make U.S. firms competitive in
the global economy / Ted Reingold.
        p.   cm. — (Garland studies on industrial productivity)
    Revision of author's thesis (Ph. D.)—Golden Gate University,
1995.
    Includes bibliographical references and index.
    ISBN 0-8153-3091-X (alk. paper)
    1. Mangement—United States. 2. Business planning—United
States. 3. Industrial policy—United States. I. Title. II. Series.
HD31.R4423 1998
658'.00973—dc21
                                                    98-9415

Printed on acid-free, 250-year-life paper
Manufactured in the United States of America

Dedicated to
my wife Patricia,
my parents Jess and Adele,
&
my sons Dylan, Scott and Jesse

Contents

Tables

Figures

Preface

Between the years 1981-1992 U.S. companies were forced to compete in a global economy. This book identifies U.S. industries and companies that were competitive during that period and highlights the management strategies and practices they used to compete successfully in the international marketplace.

Previous studies explored the issue of global competitiveness by focusing on SITC (Standard International Trade Classification) and SIC (Standard Industrial Classification) coded industries as a whole and examining the impact of government policies on competitiveness. These studies did not identify individual companies within industries nor did they analyze management strategies and practices as factors that affect competitiveness.

The basis for the results in this book came from the utilization of United Nations data available in its International Trade Statistics Yearbooks (1980-1994). The data determined the dollar value, global market share and ranking of U.S. exports and imports for all 3-digit codes within manufacturing SIT categories 5-8. Competitive 3-digit SITC categories were defined as meeting the following five criteria:

1. Having a positive trade balance at the end of the period under study.
2. Export ranking in the top ten at the end of the period under study.
3. Dollar value export growth in excess of import growth during the period under study.
4. Export market share growth during the period under study.
5. Export market share growth in excess of import market share growth during the period under study.

The empirical findings outlined in this book indicated that a significant improvement occurred in U.S. industrial competitiveness during the period 1987-1992 compared to the period 1981-1987. For the period 1981-1987 no 3-digit SITC category met all five criteria while for the period 1987-1992, forty-four 3-digit SITC categories met all five criteria. When the competitive 3-digit SITC categories were converted to 4-digit SIC codes using a conversion table provided by the National Trade Data Bank, the three largest companies (by sales) within each converted 4-digit SIC codes were identified.

The research founded that U.S. companies identified as competitive had changed their management practices and improved their manufacturing processes by being innovative, efficient, and responsive to consumer demand without government assistance. Competitive problems faced by U.S. industries had their roots in the post-WWII era (1945-1970) when companies were able to sell their products to a large domestic market with very little foreign competition and were protected by government regulations that discouraged competition and supported oligopolies. Consequently, many U.S. industries, including automobile, steel, banking and transportation did not adjust quickly to the competitive demands of the global economy.

The political and economic instability that prevailed throughout the 1970s and 1980s and the dissolution of the government-industry-labor partnership that was formed in the 1930s to the failure of major U.S. industries to compete effectively in the global economy. Scholars, government and industry leaders who call for government-corporate partnerships similar to those found in Europe and Japan and recommend the implementation of industrial policy as a means of helping American companies become competitive do not understand the core values of the American political, economic and social system. These core values have their roots in Jeffersonian democratic principles and preclude the implementation of an industrial policy.

The competitive companies identified were able to adapt management strategies and practices to meet the challenge of the global economy, which has its roots in the Information Age, not because of an industrial policy or government assistance, but because of the demand of U.S. equity markets, which severely punish companies that do not perform and factors within the U.S. culture which encourage innovation and change. The improved competitiveness of U.S. firms as chronicled in this book helped produce strong economic growth, low inflation and unemployment, bullish equity markets and political stability in the mid- and late 1990s.

Management Strategies that Make U.S. Firms Competitive in the Global Economy

CHAPTER 1

Introduction to Competitiveness

Since the rise of the Hapsburg Empire in the 1500s, the stature of nations in western civilization has been determined by their economic strength and stability, primarily because a country's economy served as the underpinning of its military power. During most of the twentieth century, the U.S. used its financial strength as a basis of its military power to dominate the world order.[1] However, advances in technology after 1970 helped reduce the importance of military strength and even contributed to the dismantling of the Soviet Union, thus greatly reducing the major military threat to the U.S. and its allies. More importantly, the technology revolution of the last 25 years has made the global economy more dynamic and important than ever before: industrial competitiveness in the world market is an important political and economic factor in determining a country's overall stature on the planet. During the period 1970-1990, as the global economic climate shifted, U.S. industrial competitiveness declined. Many of its industries lost global market share (See Table 1, Chapter 2), and its trade and budget deficits have grown (See Tables 4 and 5, Chapter 3).

Studies, by the Department of Commerce,[2] Scott and Lodge,[3] and Lenz,[4] have documented this decline of U.S. competitiveness and analyzed the factors contributing to it. These studies, which focused on Standard International Trade Classification (SITC) and Standard Industrial Classification (SIC) coded industries as a whole, did not seek to identify individual companies within competitive industries, nor did they analyze management practices and policies to determine their effect on competitiveness.

This book identifies U.S.-based industries that were competitive during the period 1981-1992. The United Nations International Trade

Statistics Yearbooks were used to determine the dollar value of exports and imports and the global market share of all U.S. 3-digit SITC manufacturing industries during the period 1980-1992. This information was then used to select 3-digit SITC manufacturing industries which increased their global market share during that period. Most data of U.S.-based companies is compiled using SIC codes; therefore, the competitive 3-digit SITC industries were converted to 4-digit SIC codes using a conversion program produced by the National Trade Data Bank. The three largest companies (by sales) within each competitive 4-digit SIC code are identified and the management practices and policies of these companies are analyzed in an attempt to determine factors that have made them competitive.

IMPACT OF TECHNOLOGY ON ECONOMIC AND MILITARY POWER

Advances in technology during the second half of the twentieth century severed the relationship between military strength, economic power, and world dominance. The development of nuclear weapons during the later stages of World War II and the technological advances that increased the destructive power of these weapons during the 1950s made these weapons both all powerful and powerless.[5] The potency of nuclear arms made it probable that their use would destroy the world as we know it. By the late 1960s, a nation's ability to develop a first strike capability seemed beyond reach. The proponents of the Star Wars System, which would create a defensive shield against nuclear attack, appeared to recognize the futility of achieving a first strike capability and supported a system that would give the U.S. military superiority through defense.

TECHNOLOGY CONTRIBUTES TO FALL OF THE SOVIET UNION

Ultimately, an inadequate economic structure was unable to maintain the powerful military and political system of the Soviet Union. However, due to the threat of the U.S.S.R. through the 1980s, military power was a primary factor in determining the overall strength of the U.S. Through numerous military alliances, the U.S. was the protector of the advanced economies of Western Europe and Asia. As the 80s ended, it became evident that despite the importance of military power, economic strength was becoming a major factor in determining a country's overall position. With technologies such as satellites, fax machines, and copiers, Soviet and Eastern European citizens were able to learn of the prosperity in the advanced European and Asian countries. The discontent fostered by this knowledge, coupled with the inability of Communist leaders to prevent their citizens from seeing, listening, and reading about uprisings in other Soviet Bloc nations, hastened the dismantling of the Communist system in Europe. Such changes have had both political and economic implications. As noted by Theodore Levitt, technology has

> Proletarianized communication, transport, and travel. It has made isolated places and impoverished peoples eager for modernity's allurements. Almost everyone everywhere wants all the things that they have heard about, seen or experienced via the new technologies.[6]

With the fall of the Soviet Union and Communist Eastern Europe, industrial European and Asian countries were freed from relying on the U.S. military. Economic factors became the primary focus in determining a nation's relative strength.

U.S. LOSES COMPETITIVE ADVANTAGE

The globalization of wants and needs resulting from advanced technologies has been reflected by growth in international trade. This growth has been caused in part by the standardization and worldwide proliferation of many products that were believed to be restricted by local or national culture.

As an indication that our economy is moving away from self-sufficiency, total U.S. exports have grown faster than the economy as a whole over the past twenty-five years, and in 1990 export expansion provided one-half of total U.S. economic growth.[7]

> U.S. imports are three times as high a share of national income as they were a generation ago. Total exports of goods and services have increased from $296.7 million in 1982 to $539.4 million in 1991 or by 81.8% and total imports of goods and services during the same period have increased from $807.1 million to $1,513.3 million or by 87.5%.[8]

Exports of principle end use commodities increased by 94.8% from 1982 -1991 while imports of principle end commodities grew by 96.6% during this same period. Standardization in industries such as autos, steel, pharmaceuticals, consumer electronics, toys, soft drinks, and fast food has made international markets critical to the current and future success of U.S. firms.

Multinational corporations were 50% more likely to survive the 1980s than domestic corporations. Profits as measured by the average pretax return on assets for multinational firms from 1986-1990, was 9% compared with 7% for domestic firms. . . . Average profits for multinationals were higher than those of their domestic counterparts in 16 of the 20 two-digit SIC industry groups.[9]

As export sales are increasing, many U.S. firms are implementing concentric growth strategies that focus on international markets. Coca-Cola, Toys 'R Us, PepsiCo, IBM, and Phillip Morris are examples of companies in diverse markets that are looking to the international arena for growth opportunities. As U.S. exports and imports have grown, the U.S. has become as dependent on international trade as Western Europe and Japan.

If you look at total trade—exports plus imports of goods and services as a share of GNP—you will find that those shares are virtually identical for the U.S., Japan and the European community taken as a group. The U.S. is now as dependent on the world economy as tiny insular Japan. That represents a stunning transformation from the situation just a couple of decades ago. In fact over the past two decades, America's dependence on the world economy has more than doubled while Japan's and Europe's have stayed about the same.[10]

Emerging technologies have changed the nature of comparative advantage; this reduction of advantage for the U.S. is a critical factor that has helped create the "near equality of the three economic super powers, the United States, Japan and an economically uniting Europe."[11] Since its inception, the U.S. has used its natural resources to increase its economic strength by focusing on high volume industries that served a relatively insulated domestic market.[12] Comparative advantage is no longer static and based on endowed natural resources, but is dynamic and can be created by policies that develop capital and technologies that enhance business opportunities.[13] Technological advances have reduced transportation and raw material costs and forced U.S. industries to compete on a basis of high value, not high volume. High value businesses effectively utilize human capital to create markets and products that solve problems.[14]

Many studies indicate that European and Asian business firms have, as a whole, been more capable of implementing business strategies and developing management practices that meet the requirements of high value enterprise. These studies note that the strategies of core competencies,[15] strategic intent,[16] and megamarketing[17] coupled with management practices of total quality management and Deming's "Concept of Quality Control"[18] have allowed many foreign based firms to gain a significant market share for their products in the U.S.[19]

CONSEQUENCES OF DECLINING U.S. ECONOMIC STRENGTH

The lessening of U.S. economic strength in the twenty-five years following World War II is considered natural by a consensus of economists and government and business leaders.

In 1950 U.S. GNP amounted to 1/3 of the total world output. By 1970 the strong growth abroad had reduced this share to some 22% of world GNP, a 35% decline. During the same period, the U.S. share of world exports declined from 21% to 18%, a proportionate drop of only 14%. The United States thus maintained its status in world trade more strongly than would be indicated by the relative size of the economy alone. Further in absolute terms, the United States has remained the world's largest single trader. In 1970, U.S. exports exceeded those of the 2nd largest exporter, Germany by 25%.[20]

The continued decline in U.S. economic strength from 1970-1990 is the primary cause of the disruption in the relationship established between business, labor, and government during the later stages of the depression of the 1930s. The modern relationship between government, business, and labor developed during the Roosevelt Administration. After World War II, this coalition was able to increase production of goods and services by implementing policies and strategies that limited risk and created a stable financial structure.[21]

Under this coalition, government was responsible for economic and social outcomes. With the support of business, the government used monetary and fiscal policies, including unemployment insurance, deficit spending, and the adjustment of interest rates, to lessen the impact of economic downturns.[22] In an attempt to effect social outcomes, the government sought to eliminate poverty through the war on poverty programs and guarantee civil rights through the Civil Rights Acts of 1964, 1965, and 1968. The federal government also attempted to lessen the burden of widowhood, old age, and disability by expanding Social Security benefits, and it acted to protect workers in the workplace by creating OSHA.

With government approval, oligopolies developed in key industries, such as steel and auto. These oligopolies created stable industrial relationships and provided a secure base that encouraged expansion to meet increased consumer demands.

Federal regulation of airlines, truck lines, telephone service, and banking created stability that helped develop a nationwide transportation and communication network and a banking system that facilitated industrial expansion.[23] Limited competitive pressure allowed companies that were regulated, or part of oligopolies, to meet increased benefit and wage packages demanded by labor unions.

> The unionized segment of the American work force declined slightly in the 1950s and 1960s but generous labor agreements nonetheless established industry-wide wage levels that continued to move steadily upward for more than a quarter century. From the end of World War II until 1973, the real wages of American production workers increased on an average of 2.5% to 3% each year. Benefits grew in tandem. In 1950 only 10% of union contracts provided for pensions, and only 30% included social insurance, five years later, 45% provided their workers pensions and 70% offered life, accident and health insurance.[24]

The success of the relationship between government, business, and labor during the twenty-five year period between 1945 and 1970 was reflected by high productivity, rising standards of living, a growing middle class, the creation of an improved infrastructure, and overall economic prosperity. As U.S. business became vulnerable to foreign competition during the 1970s, the lack of competition within the domestic business sector, expanding government social programs, and economic policies became a burden to each partner. Lack of competition in the business sector created inefficient bureaucracies and stifled innovation. Union contracts that dictated labor practices hindered the ability of business to respond to foreign competition. Inflated wage packages relative to foreign labor costs made U.S. firms vulnerable to price competition. Emphasis on financial controls at the expense of technological and organizational innovation prevented U.S. firms from formulating and implementing strategies that were needed to meet the demands of the emerging global economy.[25] During the 1970s government programs proliferated in most all areas, including welfare, social action, work safety, and the environment. "The budgets of the 42 Federal regulatory agencies grew in real terms nearly fourfold between 1970 and 1980." [26] Soon, the costs of these programs began to outrun the government's ability to pay for them. Stagnant wages resulting in part from increased foreign competition made increasing taxes politically unwise. The result was increased budget deficits.

> Budget deficits were so large that they posed a threat to the business system for generations to come. By the end of the seventies, the cumulative impact of government mismanagement of economic policy had generated severe problems for U.S. corporations operating in the domestic economy and international trade.[27]

Government regulatory statutes, including Anti-Trust laws, added to the burdens of domestic based businesses which had to compete with foreign firms operating under less stringent Anti-Trust laws. Similarly, U.S. businesses complained that federal safety, environmental, and civil rights laws hurt their ability to compete.

The disruption of the business-government-labor relationship, caused in part by the decline in U.S. economic strength, contributed to the economic and political instability of the 1970s and 1980s.

> During the 1970s Presidents Nixon (1969-1974), Ford (1974-1976), and Carter (1977-1981) each implemented a different brand of macroeconomics policy. Each failed. To combat a persistent and debilitating *stagflation*—that is, a combination of high inflation, high unemployment and a low growth rate—the government needed

to develop newer policies and apply them consistently over an extended period of time. Instead, the American government delivered bewildering successions of policies that failed to confront the underlying causes of America's economic problems.[28]

By 1980 the blame for the economic and political instability of the previous decade was placed on government.

During his presidential campaign, Ronald Reagan had repeatedly criticized government regulation of business, promising business audiences that if elected he planned to turn you loose again to do things that I know you can do so well.[29]

Reagan devoted more attention to the subject of government regulations than any previous presidential candidate.[30] As a presidential candidate, Reagan stated in September 1980,

When the real take home pay of the average worker is declining steadily and 8 million Americans are out of work, we must carefully reexamine our regulatory structure to assess to what degree regulations have contributed to this situation.[31]

During Reagan's first three years in office the economy deteriorated as the Federal Reserve continued a tight monetary policy begun in 1979. This policy caused real interest rates to rise substantially and plunged the nation into the worst recession in the post-war period.

GNP declined by 2.1% in 1982, the largest one year decline since the 1930's. More than 25,000 firms failed in 1982 and another 31,000 declared bankruptcy in 1983: the highest level of business failure since the Great Depression. High American interest rates also led to a significant increase in the value of the dollar thus increasing the nation's trade deficit. The merchandise balance of trade stood at a $25.5 billion deficit in 1980; by 1983 it increased to a $60.6 billion deficit. A year later it had doubled to $123 billion. Between 1980 and 1983 the trade deficit resulted in a shift in annual production from U.S. plants to producers overseas of roughly $50 billion worth of goods.[32]

Unemployment increased substantially from 7.5% in 1981 to 9.5% throughout 1982 and 1983. In the manufacturing sector the United States lost two million jobs between 1981 and 1984. In 1982 unemployment in the textile and apparel industries averaged 14.8% and 15%, respectively.[33]

In the early 1980s many politicians, economists, and business leaders linked the recession of 1982, the stagflation of the late 1970s, and growing budget deficits to the globalization of the world economy. They pointed to foreign competition as the reason for large trade deficits, plant closures, and high unemployment, especially in the automotive, steel, apparel, and textile industries. They began to study the factors that affected global competition, the effectiveness of U.S. industries within the world economy, and what could be done to improve competitiveness. Proposals made to address competitiveness, starting in the early 1980s, expected government to assist, not control, U.S. business. These proposals looked toward Japan, a nation where government had made helping business an important national priority.[34] Most proposals made to address this issue at that time focused on national economic planning,[35] which had its roots in the European democracies where labor had considerable influence.

In June 1983, John L. LaFalce (D-N.Y.), chairman of the Subcommittee on Economic Stabilization, announced that the committee would reexamine the nation's current tax, trade, and credit allocation programs in order to determine how they could become better suited to an increasingly competitive economy.[36] In 1984 Democrats in Congress proposed the establishment of the Council of Industrial Competitiveness to recommend strategies to enable American firms to compete more effectively. The proposal failed to reach the floor, but Congress did pass the National Cooperative Research Act that year. This Act gave anti-trust immunity to firms which formed consortia for the purpose of performing pre-competitive research and development.

COMPETITIVENESS BECOMES AN IMPORTANT ECONOMIC ISSUE

When the recession ended in 1982, the concern for U.S. competitiveness was no longer a political issue and not even mentioned in the presidential election of 1984.[37] However, academics, notably Reich, Lodge, Magaziner, Porter, and Levitt from Harvard and

Thurow and Krugman from MIT began to explore the issue. In addition, the Department of Commerce sponsored several studies and symposiums on this subject.

Trade and budget deficits grew significantly during the 1980s, and real family income increased only modestly, causing considerable public anxiety about the underlying strength of the U.S. economy and the competitiveness of American industry. This anxiety was pacified by strong, real economic growth, which averaged 3.4% between 1983 and 1988, while inflation averaged 3.8% during this same period. By the fall of 1988 the economy had approached the previous post war record for consecutive months of growth set in the 1960's.[38] The issue of competitiveness was largely confined to academic and government studies and stayed in the background. In 1990 the Persian Gulf conflict overshadowed an economic slowdown. Following the momentary euphoria of victory in the Persian Gulf, the economic downturn became the focus of national concern.

COMPETITIVENESS BECOMES A MAJOR DOMESTIC AND FOREIGN POLICY ISSUE

Just as Ronald Reagan blamed government regulations and taxes for the economic problems of the 1970s, presidential candidate Clinton in 1992 focused on a lack of U.S. competitiveness as a primary cause for economic problems. The Republicans defined the economic slowdown as a natural cyclical event. Clinton capitalized on the public anxiety caused by the budget and trade deficits and stagnant wages by defining this economic slowdown as a fundamental problem caused by a lack of U.S. competitiveness. During his campaign, Clinton proposed that the infrastructure be rebuilt and repaired, technical and general education levels be raised, an aggressive trade policy be instituted, and a government-business partnership be established to improve U.S. competitiveness. Improved competitiveness, reasoned Clinton, would create jobs, reduce unemployment, strengthen the U.S. economy, and also increase our strength in the international arena. A direct link was made between the economy and international strength. By June 1993, after only six months in office and with none of Clinton's domestic economic legislation enacted, the economy began to improve for the second quarter. Robert Dole, the Republican Leader in the Senate, declared that the Republican recovery had begun.

Despite the current economic recovery which has extended through the second quarter of 1997, U.S. competitiveness remains a major domestic and foreign policy issue. The Clinton administration, as well as most business leaders and government officials, consider U.S. competitiveness a critical factor that affects not only the U.S. economy but overall U.S. power in the world arena. The definition of competitiveness and the factors that determine and affect it are controversial. This book will begin by exploring and identifying the various definitions of competitiveness and the factors that reflect it.

NOTES

1. Paul Kennedy, *The Rise and Fall of the Great Powers*, (New York: Vintage Books, 1987), xx.

2. U.S. Department of Commerce International Trade Administration, *An Assessment of U.S. Competitiveness in High Technology Industries*, (Washington, D.C. GPO, 1983).

3. Bruce R. Scott and George C. Lodge, *U.S. Competitiveness in the World Economy*, (Boston: Harvard Business School Press, 1985).

4. Allen J. Lenz, *Narrowing the U.S. Current Account Deficit*, (Washington D.C.: Institute for International Economics, 1992)

5. Peter Drucker, *The New Realities* (New York: Harper & Row, 1989), 54.

6. Theodore Levitt, "The Globalization of Markets," *Harvard Business Review*, May/June 1983, 92.

7. Fred Bergsten, "The World Economy After the Cold War," *California Management Review*, Winter 1992, 53.

8. Paul Krugman, "Myths and Realities of U.S. Competitiveness," *Science*, November 8, 1991, 109.

9. Charles R. Taylor, "Prospering in the 90's," *Across the Board*, January/February 1992, 44.

10. Fred Bergsten, "The World Economy After the Cold War," 53.

11. Ibid., 51.

12. Bruce R. Scott and George C Lodge, *U.S. Competitiveness in the World Economy*, 93.

13. Robert Reich, *The Work of Nations*, (New York: Alfred A Knopf, 1991), 82.

14. Ibid., 84.

15. C.K. Prahalad and Gary Hamel, "The Core Competence of the Corporation," Harvard Business Review, May/June 1990, 79.

16. Gary Hamel and C.K. Prahalad, "Strategic Intent," *Harvard Business Review*, May/June 1989, 17.

17. Phillip Kotler, "Megamarketing," *Harvard Business Review*, March/April 1986, 117.

18. W. Edwards Deming, *Quality, Productivity and Competitive Position* (Cambridge, MA: MIT Center for Advanced Engineering Study, 1982), 15.

19. Fred Bergsten, "The World Economy After the Cold War," 54.

20. U.S. Department of Commerce International Trade Administration, *An Assessment of U.S. Competitiveness in History Technology Industries*, 7.

21. Louis Galambos and Joseph Pratt, *The Rise of the Corporate Commonwealth*, (New York: Basic Books, 1989), 129.

22. Ibid., 129.

23. Ibid., 178.

24. Reich, *The Work of Nations*, 56.

25. Galambos and Pratt, *The Rise of the Corporate Commonwealth*, 196.

26. David Vogel, *Fluctuating Fortunes*, (New York: Basic Books Inc., 1989), 248.

27. Galambos and Pratt, "The Rise of the Corporate Commonwealth," 206.

28. Ibid., 209.

29. David Vogel, *Fluctuating Fortunes*, 246.

30. Ibid., 246.

31. Ibid., 246.

33. Ibid., 255-256

33. Ibid., 258.

34. Ibid., 259.

35. Ibid., 259.

36. Ibid., 258.

37. Ibid., 259.

38. Ibid., 286.

CHAPTER 2

Competitiveness:
Definition and Measurement

The literature concerning competitiveness is exhaustive and wide-ranging. The following are just a few examples which either define competitiveness or identify the factors that are used to measure it.

DEFINITION OF COMPETITIVENESS

The President's Commission on Industrial Competitiveness defined U.S. International competitiveness as "The degree to which a nation can under free and fair market conditions produce goods and services that meet the test of International Markets while simultaneously maintaining and expanding the income of its citizens."[1]

The Competitive Policy Council in 1992 defined competitiveness as "a rising and sustainable standard of living for America provided by a strong growth in productivity." [2]

Robert Reich says that American competitiveness can best be defined as the "capacity of Americans to add value to the world economy and, thereby, gain a high standard of living without going into debt."[3] These definitions have been used primarily by economists with a macro or nation-as-a-whole perspective, and focus on the concepts of standard of living and productivity as the basis of competitiveness.

International competitiveness from an industry or individual firm perspective views competitiveness as "the ability to sell and profit in international markets or at a minimum compete successfully with foreign firms in the U.S. market."[4] Competitiveness from this viewpoint has also been defined as "the current and expected future ability to compete and prosper in the U.S. and international markets." [5] The industry and individual firm viewpoint assumes as Alexander Hamilton did that, "a strong manufacturing base would increase the nation's overall revenue and wealth and that a nation's citizens shared a common economic fate." [6]

The idea of economic nationalism dates back to at least the beginning of the mercantile system. The industry or individual firm concept of competitiveness is based on a revolution in the methods of manufacturing and transporting of goods that occurred between 1870 and 1900. This revolution "transformed what had been loosely knit networks of local economies into national ones, thus creating a worldwide competitive arena in which primary battles were waged nation against nation."[7]

MEASURING COMPETITIVENESS: AN OVERVIEW

The nation as a whole, or macro viewpoint, de-emphasizes economic nationalism and its zero-sum implications. It looks to the absolute prosperity of citizens as the standard for determining the health of a nation's economy and its competitiveness. The macro perspective views standard of living, or per capita consumption, as a function of productivity, and international trade as benefiting all nations, even those that produce inferior products. Citing the concept of comparative advantage developed by David Ricardo in the seventeenth century, the macro proponents note that: a nation, like a person, gains from trade by exporting the goods and services in which it has its greatest comparative advantage in producing and importing that which it has least comparative advantage.[8] Trade between nations is so much unlike competition between businesses that many macro proponents regard the word "competitive," when it is applied to countries, as dangerously misleading.[9] Macro proponents note that if U.S. productivity grows at 1%, and productivity growth in other countries was accelerating at 4%, a nation would not suffer the same losses as a company operating under that productivity lag because international competitiveness does not put countries out of business.[10]

There are equalizing forces, Krugman argues, that normally ensure that any country will remain able to sell a range of goods in the world market and balance trade on average over the long run even if its productivity, technology, and product quality are inferior to those of other nations. Even countries that are clearly inferior In productivity to their trading partners are normally better, not worse off, as a result of international trade.[11]

Macro proponents discount the individual firm or industry viewpoint and question whether global firms can provide an improved standard of living to citizens in the country the firm is identified with. Reich gives the following example: Corporation A is headquartered in the U.S. with most of its top managers, stockholders, and directors U.S. citizens. It employs mostly non-Americans in overseas locations, and much of its R&D, product design, and manufacturing is done outside the U.S.[12] Reich compares Corporation A to Corporation B that is headquartered abroad in another industrialized nation where top managers and directors are citizens of that nation and a majority of its shares are held by citizens of that nation. However, most of Corporation B employees are Americans, and it undertakes much of its R&D and new product design in the U.S. and does most of its manufacturing in the U.S.[13] Which corporation, Reich asks, adds to the living standards of U.S. citizens?[14]

FACTORS USED TO MEASURE COMPETITIVENESS— PRODUCTIVITY

Productivity of a nation's inhabitants determines where global firms will produce goods, and their productivity, not a global firm's market share, is the factor that raises the standard of living of a country's citizens.[15] The proponents of this viewpoint further note that a domestic firm wholly owned by U.S. citizens and employing exclusively U.S. citizens does not improve the nation's standard of living if it increases its profitability and market share by cutting wages of its employees and advocating import restraints and the devaluation of the dollar.

> Productivity isn't everything, but in the long run, it is almost everything. A country's ability to improve its standard of living over time depends almost entirely on its ability to raise its output per worker. World War II veterans came home to an economy that doubled its productivity over the next 25 years, as a result they found themselves achieving living standards their parents had never imagined. Vietnam veterans came home to an economy that raised

its productivity less than 10% in 15 years; as a result they found themselves living no better, and in many cases worse than their parents. Raising real consumption per capita is a function of raising productivity; real consumption per capita in the US today is about four times what it was after the turn of the century; so is productivity.[16]

The macro perspective views shifts in national power as based upon shifts in levels of productivity.

Since World War II productivity growth in Britain has averaged about 1.5% a year; in Japan it has averaged 7%. Britain won the war and Japan lost; yet Britain has become a third rank power while Japan is on the verge of becoming a first rank one.[37]

Krugman notes that the problems caused by Britain's productivity lag are not greater and, in fact, are reduced because it is a trading nation rather than a self-sufficient one.[18] Figure 2-1 reflects productivity growth in the U.S. from 1949 to1992. It shows that the average annual productivity growth (output per hour) for the business sector declined from 1949-1959 with a modest increase noted between 1989 and 1992.

Figure 2-1

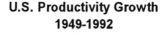

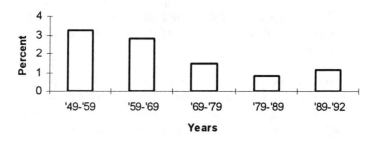

Source: Economic Report of the President 1994. Table B-48, page 323

Figure 2-2

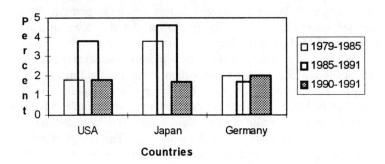

Source: Monthly Labor Review, United States Bureau of Labor Statistics, Feb. 1995, Table 1413.

Figure 2-2 compares manufacturing productivity growth rates of Germany, Japan, and the United States for the periods 1979-1985, 1985-991 and 1990-1991. The graph shows that the Japanese report higher productivity growth than the United States and Germany for the periods 1979-1985 and 1985-1991 but lower productivity growth than Germany and the US for the period 1990-1991. Macro proponents focus on the determinants of productivity growth:

> The four areas within U.S. business and government control that primarily affect productivity growth are: Capital Investment, R&D Technological Advances, Investment in Human Resources, and General Management Expertise.[19]

Proponents of the infrastructure deficit hypothesis link the decline in public capital formation that began in the 1970s with reduced productivity. It notes that this decline has also resulted in a reduced rate of return on private capital formation.[20] "In 1960 the government spent about $15 for every $100 that private industry spent for capital improvement, but by the mid-1980s that rate was halved."[21]

Although a substantial portion of capital stock is owned by the federal, state, and local governments, most of the domestic capital stock is privately owned. Growth in capital per worker is over a long period of time closely associated with labor productivity growth. From 1959 to1973 capital per worker grew by 2.0% per year while estimated overall labor productivity grew by 2.8% annually. 22 From 1979 to1991 capital per worker grew by 0.6% and productivity grew by 1.0% per year.[23] While a variety of factors may be responsible for the reported slackening of productivity growth, the slowdown in capital formation is likely to be an important one.

Private and government investment in R&D increases the stock of technical knowledge and is an important factor determining economic growth. Developments in one field often revolutionize product processes in others and increase productivity. For example, advances in computer engineering have enabled automotive manufacturers to utilize robots in the manufacture of automobiles. The growth in private R&D spending has slowed considerably since the mid-1980s and may be a factor that has reduced productivity growth. In 1988 the National Science Foundation surveyed 200 large companies that collectively accounted for 90% of industrial R&D in the United States. The survey found that overall company funded R&D remained flat or declined slightly if inflation was taken into account.[24]

Economists define human capital as the total earnings capacity of a nation's work force given the available stock of physical capital and natural resources. The level of human capital depends not only on the size of the labor force, but also on its education and experience. Improvements in the skills of the labor force through training and education directly raises productivity and living standards. "The greatest need for investment is at the lower levels—grade schools and high schools. It is here that other countries performance clearly surpasses the United States and where the greatest gains can be made."[25]

Drucker notes,

> It's management and management alone that makes effective all this knowledge and these knowledgeable people. The emergence of management has converted knowledge from social ornament and luxury into the true capital of any economy.[26]

The ability of U.S. managers to adopt strategies, policies, and practices to the global economy is a critical factor in improving productivity.

In summary:

1. Give your workers more capital to work with and a better education, and they will be more productive.[27]
2. If highways are not maintained or airlines cannot carry out schedules on time, productivity suffers. So, return the public capital stock that has been deteriorating before our eyes.[28]
3. Good management increases productivity.[29]

The U.S. recorded significant productivity gains in the early 1990s while economic growth slowed. This phenomenon caused proponents of the macro viewpoint to reexamine the relationship between productivity growth and a rising standard of living. "Since 1990 U.S. productivity has been growing at an annual rate of 2.5%, more than twice as fast as the average growth rate between 1970-1990 and markedly better than elsewhere."[30]

It is noted that the

United States lead is widest in services. Retailing is twice as productive in the United States as in Japan, where laws protect the shopkeeper from the discount chain. The fragmented American banking industry is a third more efficient than the German banking oligopolies. Gains on the factory floor have lately been even more stellar than for the economy overall. Hourly output has been rising nearly 5.0% a year for three years even as it has flattened or fallen in Germany and Japan.[31]

Efficiency achieved by improving production methods will increase productivity and improve the standard of living. The adaptation of Just in Time (JIT) production and inventory systems, which require better sales forecasting and delivery planning, will produce productivity growth and improve the standard of living. Due to product innovation, the apparel industry has been able to compete effectively against low cost foreign producers. Clothing producers are maintaining profitability through improved timing and greater flexibility of production. Foreign apparel makers typically need six months or more lead time to coordinate manufacturing with retail sales. Some domestic producers can produce products for retail more safely in three to four weeks, enabling them to set the trend with foreign producers lagging behind.

Improved quality is another factor that increases productivity and the standard of living at the same time. Superior quality wins back customers and improves sales and profits. Savings realized by avoiding the cost of reworking and repairing defects improves productivity and therefore the standard of living.[33]

Increased productivity achieved by eliminating but not replacing inefficient plants will not improve the standard of living. Productivity growth achieved by downsizing and wage cuts will not improve the standard of living either. It is noted that about half of the firms surveyed by the American Management Association downsized their operations between June 1986 and June 1987.[34]

> In 1980 the average U.S. worker in the private sector received a 9% wage boost. By 1989 the average annual increase was 1/2 of that. In some industries workers have given back prior wage and benefit increases." [35] The percentage of major corporations paying the full cost of hospitalization for their employees fell to 29% from 53% in Reagan's final term. Corporations depended more heavily on temporary workers who received fewer benefits and less pay than regular employees. Of the nearly 17 million jobs created between 1983-1989, 3 million were temporary.[36]

U.S. wages rose only 3.0% a year in current dollars between 1982 and 1990. By contrast, during this same period, wages in Germany and Japan rose 9.7% and 10.5% a year, respectively. U.S. manufacturing labor costs, per unit of output, have gone down in real inflation adjusted terms by 7% since 1982, while average labor costs for the eight other industrial countries rose during the same period. "The hourly pay of American production workers is no longer higher than that of many overseas counterparts; in many instances it is lower."[37]

It appears that productivity gains are being made at the expense of the standard of living of wage earners. Wage rates are achieving economic bipolarity as they decrease relative to wages earned by workers in other industrial countries. American workers have become subject to the "Law of Factor Price Equalization, a fancy term meaning equal pay for equal skill level."[38] The new competitive reality has especially impacted workers in companies that in the past were unusually generous in granting increases in wages and fringe benefits.

Drucker notes that the most dramatic event in this country's social history has been the rise and fall of the industrial worker:

By 1925 blue collar workers in manufacturing had been the largest single occupational group, male or female. . . . By the 1950s they and their unions had become a dominant political force in every noncommunist developed country. But in the 1970s industrial workers began to decline fast, first as a proportion of the workforce and then in numbers and finally in political power and influence.[39]

Some economists acknowledge that many efficiencies that improve productivity in the long run will in the short run displace workers, increase unemployment and hold down wage increases. However, improved productivity, these economists note, will produce an expanded economy which will increase employment, absorb displaced workers and produce a higher standard of living for everyone. Reich argues this was the case when core corporations in the immediate post war years "flooded America with goods but also created millions of jobs that swelled the ranks of America's middle class."[40] Today's competitive global economy is subject to the laws of factor price equalization and not all boats rise as the seas of productivity rise.[41]

In the 1980s increasing inequality in income distribution rather than growth in productivity was the main source of rising living standards for the top 10% of Americans. And, the 1980s was the first decade since the 1930's in which a large number of Americans actually suffered a severe decline in living standards.[42]

In 1989 the median pay of the chief executives of the nation's one hundred largest industrial firms rose about 10%. That was twice the median profit gain of the hundred firms and three times the comparable pay raise of other employees.[43]

Improvement in the infrastructure, increased spending on R&D and capital stock, and a better educated work force, economists tell us, will improve productivity. It appears that downsizing, wage cuts, and reducing the scope of operations by eliminating and not replacing old and/or inefficient plants and equipment will also increase productivity. Increased productivity growth relative to other industrial economies in the U.S.during the past several years has not increased the standard of living of all U.S. citizens, nor has it eliminated the trade deficit.

"The American worker is the most productive by far, producing an average $49,600 in goods and services a year in 1990, $5,000 more than the German workers and $10,000 more than Japanese counterparts."[44] "How can the Japanese pay wages that are higher, have productivity that is lower and still sell us $60 billion more than they buy?"[45]

The globalization of the economy is a relatively new phenomenon, and relationships between economic factors such as productivity and standard of living must be rethought and revised. Productivity is a factor that reflects standard of living and competitiveness, but not as clearly as it once did. Other factors must be examined including the trade deficit and the micro, or firm, viewpoint to better understand the issue of competitiveness in the global economy.

FACTORS USED TO MEASURE COMPETITIVENESS— TRADE DEFICIT

To most Americans the two primary factors that indicate the loss of U.S. competitiveness are (a) the foreign goods they buy and use everyday and (b) the trade deficit that is reported every month.

The merchandise trade balance measures net exports of merchandise flows. The goods and services balance measures the net exports of merchandise and service flows. The current account balance is the broadest measures of U.S. international goods and services traded. It "equals the net credits minus debits on the flow of goods, services and unilateral transfers. It also equals the change in the nation's foreign assets minus foreign liabilities, and is also known as net foreign investment."[46] It is noted that "unilateral transfers consist primarily of government outlays for foreign aid and other external grants as well as payments to U.S. pensioners living abroad."[47] The international income account records payments to foreign holders of several kinds of U.S. financial assets and payouts received by U.S. holders of similar kind of foreign assets."[48]

> Up through the 1960s the U.S. had a positive current account balance matched or exceeded by its positive trade balance. The United States was a net exporter and lender largely because Europe and Japan recovering from World War II badly needed American goods and loans. During the 1970s and up through 1982 a new pattern began to emerge. The U.S. became a net importer of merchandise but still kept its current account in balance thanks largely to interest and profit earnings in foreign investments.[49]

Figure 2-3

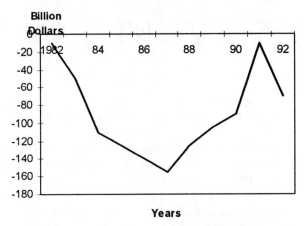

Years

Source: Economic Report of the President 1994 Table B103.

As reflected in Figure 2-3 and 2-4 the U.S. current account balance beginning in 1982 showed dramatic deficits which between 1984 and 1987 were approximately 3% of GDP. From 1988 to1992 deficits have continued to accumulate but on a whole they have been reduced in amount and as a percentage of GDP. "The current account means that the U.S. is producing less than it is consuming, importing the difference and borrowing abroad."[50]

Figure 2-4

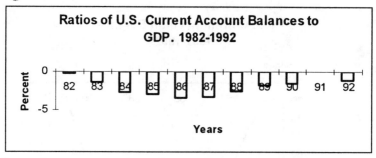

Source: Economic Report of the President 1994 Table B103

To pay for the excess imports over exports, the U.S. sells foreigners assets or debt instruments, creating the current account deficit. "The U.S. trade deficit in the 1980s was financed by a steady sale of American assets, stocks, bonds, real estate and increasingly whole corporations to foreigners."[51] Figure 2-5 shows that the U.S. went from a net positive net International Investment position at current cost of $234.2 billion in 1984 to a negative position of $521.3 billion in 1992.

Those holding a macro, or nation-as-a-whole, viewpoint of competitiveness link the federal budget deficit with the large current account and trade deficit. They argue that the budget deficit reduced national savings and that the "U.S. trade deficit was essentially caused by the fall of national savings, which led to massive imports of capital."[52] Macro proponents note that the current account and trade balance must narrow because no nation can borrow and continue to sell off its assets forever. The international economic system they note would force adjustments that would reduce borrowing abroad and thus narrow the current account deficit.

Figure 2-5

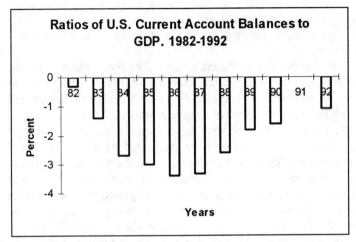

Source: Economic Report of the President 1994 Table B102, p. 385.

If the national savings rate had remained high, the loss of competitive advantage would not have led to a trade deficit. It would, instead, have led to a fall in the dollar which would have compensated for the loss of technology and quality by making U.S. goods relatively cheaper. That is what happened in the 1970s. The U.S. had about the same trade balance at the end of the 1970s as it did at the beginning, but with a much lower dollar.[53]

During the 1970s the United States exported an increasingly greater volume of goods but those goods were valued less on the world markets. In effect, U.S. products in total could not command as high a price in world markets as they once did. The decline in the value of the dollar during much of the 1970s is both a cause and a reflection of this.[54]

It is noted that the depreciation of the dollar following the Plaza Agreement in 1985 did not reduce the trade deficit which continued to rise through 1988. The trade deficit was $117.7 in 1985 and $152.1 in 1987 before falling to $109.4 in 1989.[55] Macro proponents view the trade deficit as transitory because it can be corrected by reducing the value of the dollar or through reduced borrowing from foreign countries. The consequences of such actions, many economists claim, will reduce U.S. standard of living. They point to the "collapse of foreign financing that forced Latin American economies to cut imports by 2/3 and plunged that region into a deep slump from which it still has not emerged."[56]

Clyde Prestowitz and Robert Kuttner note that "depreciating the dollar is a bad way to reduce the trade deficit, because it amounts to meeting international competition by cutting America's wages and lowering the living standards of American workers."[57]

The trade deficit is affected by currency rates and the budget deficit. It appears that it cannot be eliminated by either factor and turned into a surplus while maintaining the current standard of living until U.S.-based companies produce products that U.S. and international consumers prefer over foreign goods. It is true that a trade surplus alone is not a sure sign of a competitive economy, as evidenced by the trade surplus produced by Zaire, one of the poorest countries in the world. It is evident that foreign borrowings which help produce current account deficits cannot last forever; and when such borrowing stops, the deficits will narrow. Macro proponents view this deficit as transitory but appear to minimize the fact that the transition and its painful effect can be avoided if U.S. goods are accepted by domestic and international markets.

The trade deficit alone cannot be looked at as an indicator of competitiveness but it cannot be dismissed as not reflecting competitiveness at all. Krugman acknowledges that one solution to a trade deficit is that people must be persuaded to switch their demands from foreign to U.S. goods. He says this switch can be accomplished through imposing tariffs and import quotas or reducing the value of the dollar.[58] Producing products of quality and value is also a method of getting people to switch.

Manufacturing is a main component of the U.S. merchandise trade balance and accounts for a growing proportion of world trade in goods and services. Manufacturing is also a dominant factor in the trade performance of most industrial countries. "Manufactures trade in 1990 accounted for 80% of U.S. merchandise trade: 80.1% of exports and 78.5% of imports."[59]

FACTORS USED TO MEASURE COMPETITIVENESS: GLOBALLY-COMPETITIVE FIRMS

Proponents of a micro-level viewpoint look toward healthy firms and industries based in the home country as the basis of a competitive economy. If home-based companies, they reason, are able to compete by maintaining domestic and international market share for products they produce, then the nation as a whole will benefit. If we are not in a zero-sum contest, the micro proponents argue we are at least in an environment that has zero-sum implications where noncompetitive nations suffer consequences that are felt by their citizens.

While Robert Reich discounts the importance of a company's home base relative to the standard of living of its citizens,[60] Michael Porter notes that successful corporations usually have a distinct national identity:

> A nation's standard of living depends on the capacity of its companies to achieve high levels of productivity and to increase productivity over time. A nation's companies must relentlessly improve productivity in existing industries by raising product quality, adding desirable features, improving product technology, and boosting product efficiency. They must develop the capabilities to compete in more sophisticated industry segments where productivity is generally high.[61]

To improve productivity and the trade balance, micro proponents note that one must focus on specific industries and industry segments. Viable skills and technology are created at the firm and industry level, not on the nation-as-a-whole or macro level.

> It is the outcome of the thousands of struggles for competitive advantage against foreign firms in particular segments and industries in which products and processes are created and improved that underpins the process of upgrading national productivity.[62]

The home base is the nation in which the essential competitive advantages of the enterprises are created and sustained. It is where the company's strategy is set, where the core product and process technology is created and maintained and where the most productive jobs and most advanced skills are located.[63]

The global economy is dominated by rapid growth industries that have a high technology component. Japan in the post war years chose to use the power of government to create competitive advantage for a select group of high growth industries.

> The Japanese appear to have been the first to recognize that advantages could be created through the mobilization of technology, capital and skilled labor not just to nurture a few infant industries to supply the domestic market but as a way of nurturing the whole industrial sector towards areas of growth and opportunity in the world market.[64]

With the emergence of a form of comparative advantage that allowed for the creation of competitive advantage, non-Western trading countries created an adversarial trade policy. The concept of comparative advantage, advocated by macro proponents to support claims of the mutual benefits of international trade and discount the zero-sum implications of global economic competitiveness, is based on complementary and competitive trade.

Complementary trade of the eighteenth century sought to establish a partnership between trading partners.

> England sold wool to Portugal that Portugal could not produce while Portugal sold wine to England that England could not produce. . . .
> The entry of the U.S. and Germany into the world economy into the mid-nineteenth century brought about a shift to competitive trade. The Americans and Germans both sold chemicals and electrical machinery in competition with one another and bought chemicals and electrical machinery from each other. . .competitive trade aims at creating a customer. . . . Adversarial trade aims at dominating an industry. . . . Adversarial trade aims at winning the war by destroying the enemy and its capacity to fight.[65]

Micro proponents argue that macro analysts who promote the efficiencies brought by free trade have ignored the not-so-invisible hand of foreign governments, that have created competitive advantage and expanded that advantage through adversarial trade. Micro level advocates point to the loss of market share of many American-based companies and industries as the benchmark that reflects a loss of U.S. competitiveness.

Table 2-1 lists the twelve largest firms in the world in each of fourteen different industrial groups for the years 1960, 1970, 1980, and 1990. A ranking of countries based on the number of firms found in a particular country as well as the percentage of sales by country in relation to the group as a whole is given in *Table 2-1*.

Also, *Table 2-1* shows that U.S.-based firms had a smaller percentage of sales in 1990 in all industrial groups than they had in 1970 or 1980. In addition, fewer U.S. firms were represented in thirteen of fourteen categories in 1990 compared to 1980 and twelve of fourteen categories compared to 1970.

Table 2-1
Changes in "World Market Share" in Major Industries, 1960-1990.

Numbers of firms and percentages of consolidated sales accounted for by the twelve largest companies in each industry, by home country.

	Numbers of Firms				% of sales			
	'60	'70	'80	'90	'60	'70	'80	'90
AEROSPACE								
USA	9	9	9	9	85	88	81	79
France	0	1	2	1	3	6	5	4
UK	3	2	1	2	185	9	6	17
AUTOS AND TRUCKS								
USA	6	4	3	3	83	66	42	38
Japan	0	3	3	3	0	12	17	23
Germany	2	2	2	3	7	11	14	21
France	2	1	2	2	4	4	15	10
Italy	1	1	1	1	3	4	10	8
UK	1	1	1	0	3	4	3	0
Sweden	0	0	0	0				
CHEMICALS								
Germany	3	3	3	3	18	27	36	39
USA	8	5	4	3	68	40	31	23
UK	1	1	1	1	14	11	10	11
Italy	0	1	1	1	0	9	7	6
France	0	1	1	1	1	6	5	7

Table 2-1 continued

Norway	0	0	0	1	0	0	0	5
Japan	0	0	1	1	0	0	5	4
Netherlands	0	1	1	1	0	7	0	5

COMPUTERS/OFFICE EQUIPMENT

USA	7	9	8	6	95	90	86	70
Japan	0	1	2	4	0	3	7	23
Italy	1	1	1	1	3	5	4	4
UK	1	1	1	0	2	2	3	0
France	0	0	0	1	0	0	0	3

ELECTRICAL EQUIPMENT /ELECTRONICS

Japan	2	3	3	6	8	17	21	47
South Korea	0	0	0	1	0	0	0	11
USA	6	5	5	1	7 1	59	44	11
Germany	2	2	1	1	10	12	11	10
Netherlands	1	1	1	1	8	9	11	8
France	0	0	2	1	0	0	12	7
UK	1	1	0	0	4	5	0	0
Sweden/ Switzerland	0	0	0	1	0	0	0	7

FOOD & BEVERAGE PRODUCTS

USA	9	10	8	7	62	67	50	52
UK	1	1	3	2	24	25	36	23
Switzerland	1	1	1	1	10	8	14	15
Italy	0	0	0	1	0	0	0	6
France	0	0	0	1	0	0	0	3
Canada	1	0	0	0	4	0	0	0
Japan	0	0	0	0	0	0	0	0

IRON & STEEL

Japan	1	4	4	S	5	30	31	44
Germany	2	3	2	3	11	21	24	26
France	0	0	1	1	0	0	5	12
Australia	0	1	0	1	0	7	0	8
UK	1	1	1	1	5	12	7	6
South Korea	0	0	0	1	0	0	0	5

Table 2-1 continued

USA	7	3	3	0	74	31	26	0
Netherlands	0	0	1	0	0	0	7	0
Luxembourg	1	0	0	0	5	0	0	0

NON-FERROUS METALS

Germany	1	1	2	4	8	10	18	44
USA	8	5	3	2	63	39	21	16
France	1	2	1	1	7	19	16	13
Canada	2	2	2	2	22	18	14	12
UK	0	2	1	1	0	14	11	7
Japan	0	0	1	1	0	0	7	5
Switzerland	0	0	1	1	0	0	7	4
Belgium	0	0	1	0	0	0	6	0

NON-ELECTRICAL MACHINERY (INDUSTRY & FARM EQUIP.)

USA	5	6	5	3	37	51	41	26
Germany	4	3	2	3	42	28	23	25
Japan	0	1	1	3	0	7	6	23
South Korea	0	0	1	1	0	0	9	17
UK	0	1	1	1	0	7	5	5
France	1	0	1	1	7	0	12	5
Canada	1	1	1	0	8	6	5	0
Sweden	1	0	0	0	6	0	0	0

NON-ELECTRICAL MACHINERY (INDUSTRY & FARM EQUIP.)

USA	6	6	6	3	37	61	41	26
Germany	4	3	2	3	42	28	23	26
Japan	0	1	1	3	0	7	6	23
South Korea	0	0	1	1	0	0	9	17
UK	0	1	1	1	0	7	5	6
France	1	0	1	1	7	0	12	5
Canada	1	1	1	0	8	6	6	0
Sweden	1	0	0	0	6	0	0	0

PAPER & PAPER PRODUCTS

USA	10	9	8	7	86	81	66	62
Sweden	0	0	1	2	0	0	7	18

Table 2-1 continued

Canada	1	1	0	1	6	6	0	8
New Zealand	0	0	0	1	0	0	0	7
Finland	0	0	0	1	0	0	0	6
Germany	0	0	1	0	0	0	10	0
UK	1	2	2	0	8	14	17	0
Japan	0	0	0	0	0	0	0	0

PETROLEUM PRODUCTS

USA	10	10	7	S	77	78	61	47
Netherlands	1	1	1	1	17	16	16	18
UK	1	1	1	1	6	6	9	10
Italy	0	0	1	1	0	0	6	7
France	0	0	1	2	0	0	5	10
Brazil	0	0	0	1	0	0	0	4
Venezuela	0	0	1	1	0	0	4	4

PHARMACEUTICALS

USA	10	9	7	6	87	70	66	49
Switzerland	2	3	3	3	13	30	32	30
Germany	0	0	2	1	0	0	13	6
UK	0	0	0	1	0	0	0	9
Japan								
Sweden	0	0	0	1	0	0	0	6

TEXTILES

Japan	1	6	3	6	7	32	21	42
USA	7	6	6	3	68	44	41	21
UK	2	2	2	2	19	23	22	16
South Korea	0	0	1	1	0	0	8	11
Turkey	0	0	1	1	0	0	8	10
Netherlands.	1	0	0	0	10	0	0	0
Italy	1	0	0	0	6	0	0	0

TIRES

Japan	0	1	2	3	0	3	10	32
France	1	1	1	1	6	8	18	19
USA	6	6	7	1	76	69	50	19
Italy	1		1	1	7		9	14
UK	1	1	1	0	11	9	18	0
Germany	0	1	1	1	0	3	4	9
Australia	0	0	0	1	0	0	0	7

Source: Laurence Franko, "Global Corporate Competition II" Is the Large American Firm An Endangered Species?" Business Horizons, November-December 1991, 15.

"In 1981 manufactures trade [in the United States] was 53.2% of total trade in goods and services, but by 1990 it was 62.5% of the total."[66] Over the same period manufactures trade grew from 10.5% of U.S. GNP to 12.9%.[67] "In an integrated world economy, manufacturing is the key interface of the U.S. economy with the world economy and becomes the brunt of foreign competition."[68] The erosion of the position of U.S.-based manufacturing firms reflected in Tables 2-1 and 2-2 is used by those holding a micro viewpoint as an indicator of loss of U.S. competitiveness.

Micro proponents argue that increased sales of foreign based firms in a particular industry has zero-sum implications and hurts sales and profits of US firms in that same industry. They further note the reduced sales and profits of U.S. based firms impacts U.S. national income, wealth and standard of living. The reduced profits and sales of General Motors have caused layoffs and reduced dividends to shareholders, while increased sales and profits earned by Toyota add to Japan's wealth.

In an integrated global economy macro proponents will argue that General Motors is adding workers in foreign plants and laying off workers in the U.S. while Toyota is hiring American workers for its U.S. factories. Micro proponents note that foreign governments create competitive advantage and employ adversarial trade policies to benefit companies on their home base. These governments recognize that home-based companies have a distinct national identity and that profits generated from home-based companies help create national wealth and rising standards of living.

Reich argues that all boats do not rise in the sea of a global economy as the profits of domestic based companies rise. Robert Noyce, the founder of Intel, warns that by ignoring the concerns of firms based in the U.S., "we will find ourselves selling the farm and becoming sharecroppers."[69]

Although there is no generally accepted definition or measurement of competitiveness, there is a general consensus among scholars, industry leaders, and government officials that U.S. industrial competitiveness has declined between 1970-1990. The reasons given for the decline in U.S. industrial competitiveness fall into two broad categories: ineffective public sector policies and ineffective U.S. management strategies and practices.

NOTES

1. U.S. Department of Commerce. International Trade Commission, *Improving U.S. Competitiveness*, (Washington, D.C.: GPO, 1987), 19.

2. *The Economist*. March 7, 1992, 30.

3. Robert Reich, "Who is Us?", *Harvard Business Review*, January-February 1990, 59.

4. US Department of Commerce, International Trade Commission, *Improving U.S. Competitiveness*, 18.

5. Ibid., 18.

6. Robert Reich, *The Work of Nations*, 20.

7. Ibid., 25.

8. Bruce Scott and George Lodge, *U.S. Competitiveness in the World Economy*, 73.

9. Paul Krugman, "Myths and Realities of US Competitiveness," *Science*, November 8, 1991, 812.

10. Ibid., 811.

11. Ibid., 812.

12. Robert Riech, "Who is Us?", 53. 26

13. Ibid., 53.

14. Ibid., 53.

15. Ibid., 54.

16. Paul Krugman, *The Age of Diminished Expectations* (Cambridge, MA: The MIT Press, 1991), 9.

17. Ibid., 10.

18. Paul Krugman, "Myths and Realities of U.S. Competitiveness," 812.

19. David Altany, "The Race With No Finish Line," *Industry Week*, January 8, 1990, 105.

20. John Tatom, "Is An Infrastructure Crisis Lowering the Nation's Productivity," *Review*, November/December 1993, 4.

21. Alfred Malambre Jr., *Within Our Means* (New York: Random House, 1991), 33.

22. Paul Krugman, "Competitiveness Does it Matter?" *Fortune*, March 7, 1994, 110.

23. Ibid., 110

24. Alfred Malabre, Jr., *Within Our Means*, 65.

25. David Altany, "The Race With No Finish Line," 105.

26. Peter Druker, *The New Realities*, 223.

27. Paul Krugman, *The Age of Diminished Expectations*, 15.

28. Alfred Malabre, Jr. *Within Our Means*, 134.

29. Peter Drucker, *The New Realities*, 223.

30. Sylvia Najar, "The American Economy, Back on Top", *The New York Times*, February 27, 1994, Section 3, 6.

31. Ibid., Section 3, 6.

32. Murray Weidenbaum, "Filling in the Hollowed-out Corporation: The Competitive Status of U.S. Manufacturing", *Business Economics*, January 1990, 20.

33. Ibid., 20.

34. Ibid., 19.

35. Ibid., 19.

36. Alfred Malabre, Jr., *Within Our Means*, 113.

37. Alfred Malabre, Jr., *Within Our Means*, 114.

38. Shlomo Maital, "Future Winners", *Across the Board*, December 1991, 7.

39. Peter Drucker, *The New Realities*, 188.

40. Robert Reich, *The Work of Nations*, 48.

41. Robert Riech, "Who is Us?", 54.

42. Paul Krugman, *The Age of Diminished Expectations*, 22.

43. Alfred Malabre, Jr., *Within Our Means*, 113.

44. Sylvia Najar, "The American Economy, Back on Top", *The New York Times*, February 27, 1994, Section 3,6.

45. Ibid., Section 3, 6.

46. Peter Lindert, *International Economics*. 9th Ed (Boston: Iriwn, 1991), 333.

47. Allen J. Lenz, *Narrowing the U.S. Current Account Deficit*, 21.

48. Ibid., 21.

49. Peter Lindert, *International Economics*. 9th Ed., 326.

50. U.S. Department of Commerce, *Improving U.S. Competitiveness*, 15.

51. Paul Krugman, *The Age of Diminished Expectations*, 40.

52. Ibid., 47

53. Ibid., 47.

54. US Department of Commerce International Trade Administration, *An Assessment of U.S. Competitiveness in High Technology Industries,* 7.

55. *Economic Report of the President 1993*, (Washington D.C.: GPO, 1993) 466 Table B-103.

56. Paul Krugman, *The Age of Diminished Expectations*, 91.

57. Ibid., 99.

58. Ibid., 106.

59. Allen J Lenz, *Narrowing the U.S. Current Account Deficit*, 30.

60. Robert Reich, *Who is Us?*, 54.

61. Michael Porter, "The Competitive Advantage of Nations," *Harvard Business Review*, March-April 1990, 84-85.

62. Ibid., 85.

63. Ibid., 85.

64. Bruce R. Scott and George C. Lodge, *U.S. Competitiveness in the World Economy*, 95-96.

65. Peter Drucker, *The New Realities*, 129-130.

66. Allen Lenz, *Narrowing the U.S. Current Account Deficit*, 36.

67. Ibid., 36.

68. Ibid., 38.

69. Michael T. Jacobs, *Short Term America*, {Boston, MA: Harvard Business School Press), 1991, 5.

CHAPTER 3

The Effect of Public Sector Policies on Competitiveness

Many economists and business and government leaders have stated that fiscal, monetary, and trade policies over the past twenty-five years have contributed to stagnant living standards, declining U.S. productivity relative to other industrialized countries, large trade balance deficits, and the erosion of global market share of U.S. based industries.

Fiscal policies have been criticized for encouraging consumption and creating budget deficits. These policies have been blamed for causing high interest rates which have discouraged capital formation, hindered productivity growth, and helped create trade deficits. These policies have also been blamed for the erosion of the U.S. infrastructure, which has been linked to declines in productivity growth and the poor performance of U.S.-based industries.

Monetary policies have been blamed for pricing U.S. exports out of the world market and negatively impacting living standards. U.S. trade policies have been criticized for advancing free trade while our trading partners institute adversarial trade policies.

PUBLIC SECTOR POLICY INFLUENCES—JEFFERSONIAN DEMOCRACY

U.S. economic policy is driven by two conflicting concepts, one being Jeffersonian Democracy and the second being an Economic Security/Income Distribution philosophy. The United States' culture is rooted in the Jeffersonian Democracy of small farmers and merchants who fled oppressive governments in Europe. Jeffersonian Democracy has helped foster an individualistic ideology that emphasizes individual property rights, competition, and limited state involvement in economic activities. Vogel, as noted by Scott and Lodge, compares this individualist ideology to the communitarian ideology found in Asian societies, which emphasize rights and duties of membership in a society, consensus, community needs, and government involvement in economic activity. [1]

The size and natural wealth of the U.S. reinforced the individualist ideology.

> The economic challenge of America's early periods was straightforward, to exploit the staggering resources of a continental nation. Conquering this first American frontier demanded little but vision, daring and initiative. Ongoing collaboration was rarely needed. Distribution seems an almost empty issue.[2]
>
> Apart from its role in developing early transportation systems, government was not critical to the first stage of America's economic evolution. The government functions were few and in general were more social and cultural than economic. This pattern endured in American myth long after it had altered in fact.[3]

As business consolidated and formed national combines beginning in the 1870s, the government enacted laws that mitigated the combines' powers. These laws were enacted in response to farmers, owners of small- and medium-sized businesses, and labor leaders who feared the concentration of wealth, and power accumulated by these combines. Single industry regulation and cross industry regulation were the vehicles used by the government to respond to constituencies that demanded that combines be controlled.

Single industry regulatory agencies, including the Public Utility Commission and the Interstate Commerce Commission, were formed. They were a passive solution to the concerns of the effected constituencies because they left the property and the most important decisions about it in private hands. These agencies did not lay the foundation of an activist government.

> In the early years there was little systematic effort to analyze which sectors of the economy and which types of business were best suited for regulation. Instead, the process proceeded piecemeal in response to the demands of those, including some businessmen, who were

most effective in exerting pressure on the legislative and executive branch. Indeed there was little tendency to perceive the various regulatory agencies as parts of a whole.[4]

Cross industry regulation in the form of anti-trust laws was a response to the public's fear of monopolies. The Sherman Anti-Trust Law was not, however, the start of a plan for more government involvement. Anti-trust laws attempted to "curb the power of big business, naturally by restoring free markets without building up big government." [5]

Despite the pressure from many constituencies, government on the whole responded to its Jeffersonian roots, and has enacted laws that recognized the free market and the invisible hand. During the depression of the 1930s the government formulated policies that respected the rights of business and the limits of government power. The creation of the Security Exchange Commission, the funding of government projects, and the enactment of Banking and Social Security Laws were conservative responses to a massive economic crisis.

> Actually the New Deal's employment policies revealed as clearly as did the investment and banking programs just how deep set American concepts of a limited federal state were. The Great Depression was an unprecedented economic crisis but even that disaster could not convince most Americans of the need for an administrative state that planned and controlled business activity on a national basis. The result was a series of half-measures that softened the impact of the depression without fully committing the government to large-scale permanent jobs, programs or to a direct role in macroeconomic planning.[6]

Government's inability to form a mutually beneficial partnership with business results from an individualistic ideology coupled with a history of becoming involved in business affairs as an antagonist of business.

PUBLIC SECTOR POLICY INFLUENCES—ECONOMIC SECURITY/INCOME DISTRIBUTION

The Economic Security/Income Distribution Philosophy that currently underlies the macro economic policies of the U.S. began during the depression of the 1930s when citizens with nowhere else to turn asked the government for help. The assistance provided by the government during the depression was minimal by today's standards. Unemployment benefits were small, social security was restricted to the elderly, and modest job projects were initiated. Limited deficits relative to today were used to finance these programs. The ethic of individualism and Jeffersonian Democracy was strong and prevented many people from accepting these benefits because they believed it was their responsibility to take care of themselves.

Government, under the Economic Security/Income Distribution philosophy, "accepts an ever increasing responsibility for the income security of their citizens, for the redistribution of income and for due process in attempting to see that all citizens receive the benefits to which they are entitled."[7]

> Responsibilities are shifted away from the firm, family and individuals toward government. . . . Citizens continually expect more from the government. As a result the public sector continually assumes new roles, becoming responsible for a greater share of aggregate demand.[8]

The U.S. government's responsibility to its citizens grew from providing limited economic benefits for those suffering hardship, to entitlement programs which grew in scope and benefits. Unemployment Insurance and Social Security were expanded and a general welfare program was initiated. By the late 1970s total welfare expenditures surpassed spending on national security.[9]

To sustain domestic demand and growing social programs in time of slack economic conditions, the government, under the Economic Security Income/Distribution philosophy, will resort to deficit financing. [10] President Eisenhower in 1958 legitimized the use of deficit spending to stimulate domestic demand and maintain ongoing social programs. "When the economy became sluggish in 1957-1958 the Administration responded with a package of initiatives that increased government expenditures for defense, highway and the postal system encouraging a spurt of growth on the eve of the 1958 election." [11] These expenditures produced significant budget deficits but did not satisfy an electorate that was unhappy with the "Eisenhower recession." The Republicans lost 13 seats in the Senate and 48 seats in the House in the 1958 off year election.[12] The dichotomy between the Jeffersonian philosophy that encourages government to maintain a laissez faire approach toward economic matters and the Economic Security/Income Distribution philosophy that demands that government provide a risk-free economic and social environment for all its citizens is a conflict that produces confused and sometimes resentful citizens. The conflict produces citizens similar to the petulant child who wants nothing to do with his/her parents but demands they protect him/her and in the end resents them.

Many economists, business leaders, and government officials look toward government fiscal, monetary, and trade policies and its invisible-hand approach toward critical industries as factors contributing to the loss of U.S. competitiveness. The conflict between the Jeffersonian democracy philosophy and Economic Security/Income Distribution philosophies must be recognized as the underlying factor that influences government macroeconomic policies and government business relations.

FISCAL POLICIES

The five components of the U.S. budget for the years 1976, 1985 and 1993 and the budget deficits incurred during those years are shown in Table 3-1. Table 3-1 shows that defense spending has increased by 325% since 1976 but that its percentage of the total budget has decreased from 24.10% in 1976 to 20.7% in 1993. Social programs have increased by 406% and their percentage of the budget grew from 54.8% in 1976 to 58.8% in 1993. The largest percentage increase was in the interest paid on the increasing budget deficit. Interest expense has grown by 745% since 1976, and its percentage of the budget has grown from 7.2% in 1976 to 14.1% in 1993.

The increase in the budget, at least in part, is based on the Economic Security/Income Distribution philosophy which advocates the expansion of social and economic programs that will ensure economic security for all citizens. Figure 3-1 shows the projected real growth rates of principal Federal Budget components for fiscal 1994-1998. It projects that health care entitlements, Social Security, and Net Interest are the only components that will have annual average percentage increases during this period.

Table 3-1

Major Components of U.S. Budgets (in Billions of Current U.S. Dollars)

	1976		1985		1993	
Outlay	$	%	$	%	$	%
Defense	89.6	24.1	252.7	26.7	291.1	20.7
Social Programs	203.6	54.8	471.8	49.9	827.5	58.8
Interest	26.7	7.2	129.5	13.7	198.8	14.1
International	6.4	1.7	16.2	1.7	16.8	1.2
Other	45.5	12.2	76.2	8.0	74.0	5.2
Total	371.8	100.0	946.4	100.0	1408.2	100.0
Deficit	-73.7		-212.3		-254.7	

Executive Office of the President, Office of Management and Budget
Budget of the United States Government Historical Tables, Fiscal Year 1995,
(Washington, DC: GPO, 1994), Table 3-1, 40-42, Table 1.3, 17.

Figure 3-1

Projected Real Growth Rates of Principle Federal Budget Components for Fiscal Period 1994-1998

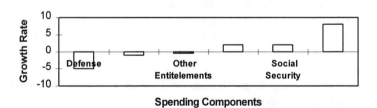

Spending Components

Source: Economic Report of the President 1994, Unit 1-10, p. 49.

Table 3-2 shows that deficits as a percentage of GDP have not increased since 1986. Table 3-3 shows that a large structural deficit remains built into the budget, ensuring that deficits will continue to be incurred and interest payments will continue to rise. The political and economic effect of the budget deficit and its impact on competitiveness is reflected in statements made in numerous congressional hearings during the late 1980s and early 1990s. The following remarks were made by Senator Orrin Hatch (A-Utah) during a hearing before the Subcommittee on Deficit, Debt Management, and Interest Debt of the Senate Finance Committee on June 5, 1992:

> The deficit has become one of the top priorities for American citizens. And we have seen several of our colleagues return citing the frustration of Congress' inability to deal with the problem. And in a recent poll conducted in my home state of Utah, Utahans listed the deficit and budget problems as the Number 2 national concern behind the current recession. The problem of the deficit, as we all know is not a new one. In the last 30 years, the Federal Government has had a surplus for only one of the last thirty years. Not only have we run deficits but the deficits have grown substantially. . . . The cumulative result of these deficits Is an outstanding Federal Debt of nearly $4 Trillion. The interest on this debt tripled in the last thirty years growing from 6% of taxes to over 18%. . . . These deficits are draining national savings and putting a strain on private sector productive investment. We have seen spending in areas such as research and development, human capital and plant and equipment decline as a result of the huge share of available capital that is siphoned into the public sector. For the most part, these siphoned funds are used to service the interest on the debt. Therefore, the public sector is not investing in the important areas. . . . While we may escape the serious consequences of our actions, our children and grandchildren will be sentenced to a lower standard of living and a nation with less ability to compete in the international economy. We must do something to reduce the deficit and give the future generations of Americans the chance for economic growth and international competitiveness.[13]

Table 3-2

Deficit as % of GDP (in Billions of Current U.S. Dollars)

	Deficit	GDP	Deficit/GDP %
1986	221.2	4219.0	5.2
1987	149.8	4452.4	3.4
1988	155.2	4808.4	3.2
1989	152.2	5173.3	2.9

Table 3-2 continued

1990	221.4	5481.5	4.0
1991	269.5	5673.3	4.8
1992	290.4	5937.2	4.9
1993	254.7	6294.8	4.0
Avg. 1986-1993	214.3	5255.0	4.1

Executive Office of the President, Office of Management and Budget
Budget of the United States Government Historical Tables, Fiscal Year 1995,
(Washington, DC: GPO, 1994), Table 12, 18, Table 1.3, 17.

Table 3-3

Structural Budget Deficits

	Structural Deficits	
Fiscal Year	Billions of Dollars	Percent of GDP
1992	206	3.5
1993	214.4	3.4
1994	190.8	2.9
1995	149.1	2.1
1996	156.1	2.1
1997	162.8	2.1
1998	171.4	2.1

Source: Economic Report of the President 1994, Table 1-6.

During the same hearing, Senator Bill Bradley, (D-New Jersey) noted,

> Large federal deficits absorb an alarming percentage of our national
> savings pool. It is the pool that provides capital for investments by
> the private sector. Such investment is critical to maintaining our
> productivity growth rate. [14]

During the hearings Mr. Bowsher, Comptroller General, U.S.
General Accounting office stated that:

> From 1960-1969 we used about 2% of net national savings for
> financing the federal debt. In the 1980s deficits absorbed 48% of the
> savings and in the 1990s, it was running at 58%. . . . Reduced savings
> reduces productivity because it reduces the stock of machines

housing and other structures available to American workers. As productivity falls, real wages, therefore falls and the standard of living is lower in the future. [15]

Rudolph Penner, the Director of Economic Studies and Policy Economic Group for KPMG Pete Marwick notes that:

> Foreigners will replace some of the American savings destroyed by the budget deficit. Consequently investment worker productivity and future standard of living will be reduced less because of our ability to draw on foreign capital. The United States will have to pay interest and dividends on the money invested by foreigners and this will be a drain on the living standards of our children. [16]

Robert Reischaurer, Director of the Congressional Budget Office, indicates, "Raising federal deficits would not adversely affect growth if they financed productive investment in such things as infrastructure and education." [17] However, because of a priority toward consumption and social programs, federal investment as a share of GDP in constant dollars has fallen slightly over the last twenty years.[18] Mr. Reischaurer notes "the unfortunate fact of the past decade and a half has been that we are running these very high budget deficits to finance consumption, current consumption. And future generations may not be so willing to bear the burden of that." [19]

> By influencing how much and where people work, save and invest, taxes also help determine how efficiently society uses all its resources and how much of those resources are devoted to investment for the future.[20]

The tax policies on a whole have favored consumption with the tax burden primarily on savings and investments. Full interest deductions on first mortgages and home equity loans stimulate the real estate market and encourage consumption. Senator Bradley noted that the elimination of the mortgage deduction would produce $31 billion in additional revenue in 1993 and $253 billion in revenue for the five year period 1993-1997. [21]

A stimulated real estate market does not improve U.S. global competitiveness; increased consumption stimulates imports and adds to the U.S. trade imbalance. Taxes on savings interest and dividends, no investment tax credit, and tax allowance for capital gains do not provide incentives to save and invest, which would enhance future output and productivity by encouraging capital formation.

In a 1985 hearing before the Subcommittee on Economic Goals and Intergovernmental Policy, Representative Fielder asked Donald Peterson, Chairman and CEO of Ford Motor Company, if the investment tax credit and accelerated cost recovery depreciation system had any impact whatsoever in making the auto industry more competitive. Mr. Peterson responded,

> What happened in 1981 was extremely helpful. Indeed, it very clearly helped us make major investments. We invested billions of dollars while we were losing billions of dollars and it helped us greatly to make those very investments in new products and new facilities that permitted us to achieve the improvement in our competitiveness.[22]

Reischaurer concluded, however, that "tax reform is unlikely to offer as large an opportunity for enhancing long term growth as would be gained by simply reducing Federal borrowing, and in that way increasing national savings." [23]

Personal consumption as a percentage of GDP rose from 66.7% in 1987 to 68.5% in 1990 while Gross Private Domestic Investment fell from 16.8% of GDP in 1986 to 13.5% in 1990. Japan's nonresidential investment in 1992 was 20.7% of its GDP. Since 1987 the U.S. has invested a smaller share of GDP in plants and equipment than any other industrialized country. [24]

The Economic Security/Income Distribution philosophy underlying the welfare state makes a commitment of economic security for all, not just the poor. The bulk of the budgetary cost for the welfare state in all industrial countries operating under the Economic Security Income Distribution philosophy comes in two programs that are not means tested: retirement and medical care.

Reischaurer stated that the growth of outlays of government health care and social security benefit programs was the primary reason for the projected future deficits. [25]

Eugene Steuerle, a senior fellow representing the Urban Institute, indicates that the growth of entitlements, which are programs that can be cut only by explicit legislation, has eliminated fiscal slack.

The entitlements and budget deficits have prevented a reallocation of budget expenditures in response to changed needs and priorities. R&D and education are two key factors that promote growth and have had their appropriations reduced as a percentage of the budget.[26]

Macro proponents including Robert Parring, the President and Chief Executive Officer of the Federal Reserve Bank of San Francisco, identify the budget deficit as the source of the current account deficit. "Reduced domestic savings and investment caused by the budget deficit have forced the U.S. to borrow from abroad, contributing to the current account deficit." [27] The projections of continued budget deficits reflected in Figure 3-2 cause macro proponents to predict continued current account deficits. The relationship between the budget deficit and current account deficit from 1982 to 1992 is shown in Table 3-4. It appears that between 1982 and 1986 the Budget and Current Account Deficit both increased. However, since 1987 the relationship does not show a clear pattern.

Figure 3-2

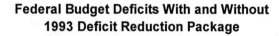

Federal Budget Deficits With and Without 1993 Deficit Reduction Package

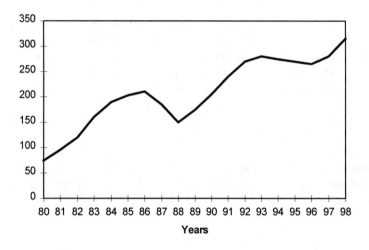

The Merchandise Trade Balance is the largest component of the current account balance. Table 3-5 shows that it has been the major factor that has contributed to deficits recorded in the current account balance. Improvement in the Merchandise Trade Balance is the key to improvement in the current account balance; 80% of that balance is accounted for by manufactures trade.[28]

Table 3-4
Budget Deficit and Current Account Deficit 1982-1992
(Billions of Dollars)

Year	Budget Deficit	Current Account Deficit
1982	127.9	11.4
1983	207.8	44.4
1984	185.4	100.3
1985	212.3	123.8
1986	221.2	150.2
1987	149.8	167.3

Table 3-4 continued

1988	155.2	127.2
1989	152.5	101.6
1990	221.4	91.9
1991	269.5	8.3
1992	290.4	66.4

Source: Economic Report of the President 1994 Table b-78, p. 360-361 and Table b-103, p. 386.

INEFFECTIVE TRADE POLICIES

Proponents of the micro viewpoint, including many business and government leaders, identify the Free Trade policies of the U.S. government as a factor contributing to the Merchandise Trade Deficit. In hearings before the Subcommittee on Economic Goals and Intergovernmental Policy in September 1985 the following concerns were voiced:

Donald Peterson, Chairmen of the Board and Chief Executive Officer of Ford Motor Company stated, "The U.S. must continue to insist on improved access to overseas markets for U.S. products equal to the access we accord our trading partners. It is not enough to rely on technology and innovation to keep us ahead." [29]

Table 3-5
Current Account Deficit and Merchandise Trade Deficit 1982-1992
(Billions of Dollars)

Year	Current Account Deficit	Merchandise Trade Deficit
1982	11.4	36.5
1983	44.4	67.1
1984	100.3	112.5
1985	123.8	122.2
1986	150.2	145.1

Table 3-5 continued

1987	167.3	159.6
1988	127.2	127
1989	101.6	115.2
1990	91.9	109
1991	8.3	73.8
1992	66.4	96.1

Source: Economic Report of the President 1994 Table b-78, p. 360-361 and Table b-103, p. 386.

Senator Lloyd Bentsen noted, "Free trade to me presupposes that you are going to have some reasonable balance of trade. Without that, I don't see how we can have a continuous drain from this country without finally hurting the standard of living of our people."[30]

Paul Davidson, Professor of Economics at Rutgers indicated, "Free trade is not a goal in itself. It is a means to an end which requires certain preconditions. These include full employment of the trading partners and a balance of trade so that there are no cash flow problems. . . Free trade cannot be an overriding guiding principle in the absence of full employment, particularly if large trade deficits occur."[31]

Representative Jim Wright, in a hearing before the Task Force on Economic Policy of the Committee on the Budget held during October 1985, linked the trade and budget deficits by noting that the trade deficit

> reflects the closing of thousands of plants and the loss of hundreds of thousands of highly skilled high wage manufacturing jobs. . . These trends aggravate the budget deficit by both decreasing the income tax revenue and increasing the necessary outlays for counter recession measures.[32]

During this committee hearing, scores of examples of lost jobs and plant closings in a wide range of industries resulting from foreign competition were reported. For example, foreign suppliers' control of the U.S. steel market was reported to have increased from 15% in 1979 to 28% in 1989, the foreign share of the United States tv and radio market rose from 43% to 60%, and the foreign share of U.S. telephone equipment market jumped from 7% to 21% during this same period. Job losses of 200,000 in the steel industry and 45,000 in the tire industry were blamed on international competition.[33]

These hearings produced the International Economic Reform Act of 1986, which was introduced by Jim Wright in May of that year. The bill covered a wide range of trade competitive issues including an export financing program, increased funding for education, job training and research, and the Gephart Amendment.

> The so called Gephart Amendment, which mandated import restrictions on countries whose excessive trade surpluses were caused by unjustified or discriminatory trade practices, quickly became the most controversial aspect of the bill. Under this formula at least four countries would be singled out for retaliatory action Japan, South Korea, Taiwan, and West Germany.[34]

This bill took over two years to get through Congress and was vetoed by President Reagan in 1988. Congress passed and the President signed in 1988 the Omnibus Trade and Competition Act which attempted to correct trade imbalances particularly with Asian industrial nations. The Act included a provision similar to the Gephart Amendment known as Super 301. The provision required that the U.S. Trade Representative (USTR) designate foreign countries that have erected barriers to U.S. exporters. Under the provision, the USTR was first to open talks in an attempt to negotiate the removal of trade barriers. If within three years, agreement was not reached, retaliatory measures including a tariff of up to 100% would be imposed. The Act specifically targeted Japan and required the USTR to immediately initiate investigation of Japanese trade barriers.[35]

In 1989 the Bush Administration invoked Super 301 against Japan, accusing them of erecting barriers to American processed wood products, supercomputers, and satellites. Japan opened the market for all three before retaliatory measures took effect. *The New York Times* reported in 1994 that Japan has performed well in these three areas since 1989.[36] In 1990 the Bush Administration let the 301 provision lapse. President Clinton, responding to a $59.3 billion trade deficit with Japan in 1993 and citing no progress in negotiations to reduce the deficit, signed an executive order in March 1994 to reactivate Section 301.[37] It appears that after twenty-five years of trade deficits the U.S. is becoming more aggressive in demanding that foreign countries open their markets to U.S. products.

Many economists and government officials indicate that the reluctance to limit free trade in the face of trade deficits stems from the consequences of the Smoot-Hartley Tariff Act of 1930. In 1930, our leading trading partners erected tariffs against American goods in response to this act . As a result, international trade was reduced and worldwide economic conditions worsened. Free trade is cited by many scholars and business, and government officials as helping produce the post World War II economic recovery of the non-Communist world, especially in Japan and Western Europe. It is also cited as contributing to U.S. prosperity during the 1950s and 1960s. In an economy where consumption is an important priority, free trade benefits consumers by increasing competition, which helps moderate prices and improves the quality of products available for sale.

The executive branch advocated a free trade policy during the 1980s despite unfair trade practices documented by Congress and other government agencies. These practices included dumping of semiconductors by Hitachi to gain market share, targeting of selected industries by foreign governments, predatory export financing by the Brazilian aircraft industry, and quotas set by foreign governments on U.S. products. The executive branch did respond to these practices when pressured by the effected industry groups or when Congress threatened to pass legislation that would restrict trade and protect U.S. jobs threatened by foreign competition.[38]

During this time voluntary export quotas were negotiated to protect the U.S. automobile and steel industries. Also, during this period an International and Multifiber Agreement was created by the international community in part to assist the U.S. textile industry. The government did provide subsidies for agricultural products and imposed tariffs on large motorcycles to assist Harley Davidson.[39]

Many scholars and government leaders note that failure of the U.S. government to respond to the adversarial trade policies of foreign governments is the result of an ineffective structure within the executive branch. The 1974 Trade Act created the cabinet rank Office of the Special Trade Representative to coordinate and preside over trade negotiations. Critics note the following:

1. The government trade operation is unwieldy with 25 different federal agencies involved in trade policy and export programs.[40]
2. No one knows where the trade buck stops, at the Department of Commerce or the United States Trade Representative, (USTR) and neither trade agency has a strong industry sector analytical capability.[41]
3. The structure does not exist for turning industry data into information that can aid in the development of trade policies.[42]
4. In addition to structural problems U.S. trade negotiators do not have attractive career paths, which leads to excessive turnover and a lack of expertise.[43]
5. In addition many U.S. negotiators take high paid positions with foreign competitors and use their knowledge against U.S. trade interests.[44]

The U.S. provides less assistance to domestic companies involved in foreign trade than their trading partners do. U.S. industries normally receive protection against exports only when imports are dumped or subsidized. . . . However, U.S. law and practice regarding subsidies and dumping by and large fail to compensate for the advantages foreign governments create for their firms.[45]

Nearly all industrial nations promote exports. . . . Governments help firms learn about potential foreign markets, identify potential customers and provide export financing. However the U.S. spends far less promoting manufacturing exports than many of its trading partners.[46]

"In the U.S., applications for financing assistance for manufacturing exports must be justified on a case-by-case basis; the need for justification increases delay and the burden on the exporter."[47] Japan and most European countries employ a broad policy that specifies what exports will obtain assistance and all that creditworthy exports meeting the guidelines qualify for that assistance.

Some economists note that the U.S. today is a large enough market with enough power that it could impose tariffs without retaliation from its trading partners. They suggest that the U.S. optimum tariff is well above current levels, probably about 50%.

The lack of an aggressive trade policy is cited by many government and business leaders as a significant factor contributing to the merchandise trade deficit. The inability of government and business to develop a cooperative working relationship is the underlying factor that has contributed to an ineffective foreign trade structure and policy. It appears that U.S. policy up until now has not been able to force foreign governments to open markets for U.S. goods nor has it assisted U.S. industries in their exporting efforts, relative to the assistance that foreign governments provide their home based industries.

Because the U.S. is now nearly as dependent on international trade as Japan and a uniting Europe, many economists, and government officials view trade policy as less important than fiscal or monetary policy in determining industrial competitiveness.

MONETARY POLICIES

Monetary policy affects competitiveness because it influences the value of the dollar, which in turn determines the price of American exports abroad and the cost of imports to the U.S. An increase in the value of the dollar relative to other currencies makes U.S. exports more expensive relative to similar goods manufactured abroad and makes imports cheaper.

In order to combat the high inflation rates experienced in the late 1970s, Paul Volker, chairman of the Federal Reserve, in 1979 began raising interest rates and tightening monetary policies. His policies broke the inflation cycle of the 1970s but contributed to the 1981-1982 recession, the most severe recession since the depression of the 1930s. The combination of the tax cuts of 1981, the reduction of interest rates and an increase in the money supply in 1982 stimulated the economy and helped produce a recovery by 1983. The Federal Reserve raised interest rates in 1984 to prevent renewed inflation from accompanying the recovery. The increase in U.S. interest rates put them well above the rates of other industrial countries, attracted foreign funds to the U.S., and helped raise the value of the dollar. While foreign funds helped offset a reduction in domestic savings caused by the budget deficit, the increased value of the dollar adversely effected U.S. exports and helped increase the trade deficit. "The increased value of the dollar gained its own momentum and by 1985 its value could not be explained by fundamentals such as interest rate differentials."[48]

Fred Bergsten in a statement before the Subcommittee on Economic Goals and Intergovernmental policy in March 1985 stated,

> The dollar is now overvalued in terms of the underlying trade competitiveness of the United States by about 40%. We are taxing all our exports by about 40% and we are providing a subsidy of about 40% on all goods coming into this country competing with American farmers, workers and firms and therefore pricing ourselves out of many markets.[49]

Bergsten recommended that the administration reverse its stand supporting a strong dollar and make a strong statement that the Administration, the Federal Reserve and Congress will make policy decisions necessary to lower the exchange rate for the dollar.[50] The only other alternative Bergsten gave at the time was a protectionist policy that would slow the amount of imports coming to this country.

The combination of a strong dollar and a budget deficit helped produce a current account deficit of $100 billion in 1984 and helped turn the U.S. into a debtor nation from the largest creditor two years before. In September 1985 the G-7 nations implemented the Plaza Agreement which established a policy of reducing the value of the dollar. The 20% devaluation of the dollar after the G-7 meeting is credited by many economists with helping increase non-agricultural exports by an average annual rate of 20% between 1987-1989, compared to a 2.1% annual average increase between 1981-1987.[51] Non oil import growth slowed from 10.5% between 1980 and 1987 to 7.5% between 1987 and 1989.[52] The fluctuation of the dollar prior to and after 1985 indicates that the

> real economy of goods and services no longer dominates the transnational economy, the symbol economy of money and credit does. ... Ninety percent or more of the transnational economy's financial transactions do not serve what economists would consider an economic function. They serve purely financial functions. These money flows have their own rationality, of course, but they are in large part political rationality's: anticipation of government decisions as to central bank interest rates or foreign exchange rates, tactic, government deficits and government borrowings or political risk assessment.[33]

Drucker's statement casts doubt on the ability of government to influence the value of currencies in the future as they did in the past.

CONCLUSION

The depreciation of the dollar was an important factor in reducing the trade deficit between 1987 and 1989 because it helped stimulate exports by making them cheaper and slowed the growth of imports by making them more expensive. However, the merchandise trade deficit is still in excess of $100 billion. Some economists believe that the dollar should depreciate further by another 15% to help reduce the deficit even more. Other economists and government officials believe further depreciation will not significantly reduce the trade deficit because other factors, including government trade and fiscal policies, are involved. Micro analysts believe that firm level competitiveness underlies the current merchandise trade deficit.

NOTES

1. Bruce R. Scott and George C. Lodge, *U.S. Competitiveness in the World Economy*, 121.

2. Robert Reich, *The Next American Frontier*, (New York: Times Books, 1983), 7.

3. Ibid., 7.

4. Louis Galambos and Joseph Pratt, *The Rise of the Corporate Commonwealth*, 47.

5. Ibid., 57.

6. Ibid., 13.

7. Bruce Scott and George Lodge, U.S. Competitiveness in the World Economy, 106.

8. Ibid., 106-107.

9. Louis Galamos and Joseph Pratt, *The Rise of the Corporate Commonwealth*, 212.

10. Bruce R. Scott and George Lodge, *U.S. Competitiveness in the World Economy*, 108.

11. Louis Galambos and Joseph Pratt, *The Rise of the Corporate Commonwealth,* 135.

12. *The New York Times,* October 2, 1994, 1.

13. Congress, Senate, Committee on Finance, Subcommittee on Deficit, Debt Management and International Debt, *Long-Term Impact of the Federal Deficit on the US Economy*, June 5, 1992 (Washington D.C.: GPO, 1992), 3-5.

14. Ibid., 2.

15. Ibid., 5.

16. Ibid., 82-83.

17. Ibid., 87.

18. Ibid., 87.

19. Ibid., 29.

20. Ibid., 88.

21. Ibid., 49.

22. Congress Subcommittee on Economic Goals and Intergovernmental Policy of the Joint Economic Committee, *Economic Effects of Trade Legislation*, September 18, 1985 (Washington D.C. GPO, 1985) 9.

23. Congress Senate, Committee on *Long-Term Impacts of the Federal Deficit in the U.S. Economy*, 88.

24. Daniel F. Burton Jr. "High Technology Competitiveness", Foreign Policy, Fall 1993, 118.

25. Congress Senate, *Long-Term Impact of the Federal Deficit on the U.S. Economy*, 90.

26. Ibid., 94.

27. Robert Parring, "U.S. Trade Deficit and International Competition", *Business Economics*, January 1994, 22.

28. Allen J. Lenz, *Narrowing the U.S. Current Account Deficit*, 2-30.

29. Congress, *Economic Effects of Trade Legislation*, 4.

30. Ibid., 7.

31. Ibid., 17.

32. Congress House, Task Force on Economic Policy of the Committee on the Budget, *International Trade and the Federal Deficit*, October 19, 1985, (Washington D.C. GPO, 1985), 2.

33. Ibid., 2.

34. Don Bonker, *America's Trade Crisis*, (Boston: Houghton Mifflin Company), 1988, 68.

35. *The New York Times*, March 4, 1994, A1.

36. Ibid., D2.

37. Ibid., D2.

38. Don Bonker, *America's Trade Crisis*, 62-63.

39. Ibid., 63.

40. Ibid., 148-149.

41. Ibid., 149.

42. Ibid., 149.

43. Ibid., 151.

44. Ibid., 151.

45. "Competing World Economies", *Congressional Digest*, December 1992, 295.

46. Ibid., 245.

47. Ibid., 295.

48. Robert Blecker, *Beyond the Twin Deficits* (Armonk, NY: M.E. Sharpe, 1992) 44.

49. Congress, Joint Economic Committee. Subcommittee on Economic Goals and Intergovernmental Policy, *Impact of the Dollar on U.S. Competitiveness*, March 12, 1985 (Washington D.C. GPO, 1985) 53.

50. Ibid., 54.

51. Fred Bergsten, *International Adjustment and Financing*, (Washington D.C.: Institute for International Economics, 1991), 16.

52. Ibid., 16.

53. Peter Drucker, *The New Realities*, 127.

CHAPTER 4

The Effect of Management Policies on Global Competitiveness

Micro proponents focus on management policies and practices of individual firms and industries when analyzing a nation's competitiveness. Micro analysts define competitiveness as "the ability of a firm to meet and beat its rivals in supplying a product on a sustainable (long-term) and viable, (profitable) level."[1]

Ineffective U.S. corporate management policies—and the strategies, structure, administrative procedures and production systems that evolve from these policies—have been blamed for the loss of market share in mature and technology-based industries for the period 1970-1990.[2] International competition and unprecedented advances in technology made these policies, effective since the early 1900's, ineffective by the 1970s.

THE SUCCESS OF U.S. MANAGEMENT STRATEGIES AND PRACTICES 1870-1970

National combines were formed from networks of local businesses within the same industry beginning in the 1870s. These combines increased labor efficiencies and facilitated vertical growth by installing a functional structure that required a high degree of functional specialization.

The highest position in each function was that of vice president, and all vice presidents served in the central office. Directly under them were the department directors who ran operations on a day-to-day basis. Performance in these positions and those down the line could be carefully measured because each manager had a designated area of responsibility, an area whose output and costs were recorded and evaluated regularly by the head of the departments.[3]

This structure fit nicely into the ethos of Frederick Taylor's Scientific Management Theory and placed new emphasis on cost accounting. It also helped eliminate bottlenecks and inefficiencies, poor coordination, and inadequate controls. The success of the vertical growth strategy and the functional structure that allowed its implementation is reflected in the concentration of production that large manufacturing firms controlled. By 1929 the top 10% of firms produced 77% and the top 20% of firms produced 88.1% of the total value of manufactured goods produced.[4]

The functional structure was dominant until the end of World War II when companies began to diversify. Pent up demand resulting from the depression, sacrifices made, and personal savings accumulated during the war, encouraged U.S. firms to expand their operations and look beyond industries in which they were already established. Diversification into related products and services linked by a common technology or by a common form of marketing became a popular strategy.

> Decentralization and diversification basically transformed the American Business setting. . . . They freed the corporation from the limits of a single industry growth path and the seemingly inevitable curve of the product cycle. Now a corporation could renew itself by edging into entirely new industries or new market areas around the nation or for that matter around the world.[5]

The divisional structure was developed to allow for the successful implementation of the diversified strategy. The divisional structure organized functional departments into divisions handling related product lines.

> Over all these divisional lines of business was a central office that performed the basic function of allocating the firm's resources and supervising in a general way the performance of the divisions. Day-

to-day operations were left in the hands of the divisions; power was clearly decentralized. Major entrepreneurial decisions were made by the CEO and executive committee; maintenance of efficiency and a good profit performance were largely divisional responsibilities.[6]

The divisional structure allowed corporations to expand their operations across product lines and geographical areas. Dupont could effectively manage its gunpowder and artificial leather product divisions; Sears & Roebuck divided its operations into regions; and Standard Oil used the divisional structure to direct its worldwide operations.[7]

> Business enterprises that standardized and coordinated their work achieved spectacular efficiencies. Management hierarchies that emphasized sophisticated techniques to supervise and monitor subordinates gained a cost advantage over their competitors. Real advantage lay in the relative efficiency with which inventories and resources were managed.[8]

The success of centralized and diversified strategies was a key factor in creating American industrial domination, economic prosperity, and stability for the first seventy years of the twentieth century, particularly between 1945 and 1970.

Government policies after World War II encouraged business stability, which reduced risk and encouraged investments. Businesses needed to invest large amounts of capital to expand their operations, especially in capital-intensive industries like autos, steel, rubber and petrochemicals. Oligopolies were formed in major sectors of the economy and helped create stable prices and market share. These oligopolies were not challenged by anti-trust laws. Regulatory laws governing utilities, banking, transportation, and communication essentially outlawed price competition and discouraged new businesses from entering the marketplace.

> As a result of these policies large business organizations achieved an extraordinary stability from 1920-1970. . . . Of the 278 largest industrial companies in 1920 only 14 had been liquidated, dissolved or discontinued during this period. . . . Half of America's 50 largest manufacturing companies in 1947 were still within the top 50, 25

years later. The other half were still in the top 200 . . .All but 5 of America's 50 largest manufacturing companies in 1972 were among the top 200 in 1947.[9]

Just as the same firms dominated industries, so the same industries dominated the American economy as a whole throughout this period. In 1920 and in 1970, 22 of the 200 largest companies were in petroleum, 5 of the 200 largest at both ends of the era were in rubber; 18 in machinery; 20 in food products; and 20 in transportation equipment. . . . The same set of industries (with the addition of electronics and aircraft, which were just emerging in 1920) led the economy in technological advances, the production of capital goods and wages.[10]

Management policies in the twenty-five years following World War II helped create economic growth, jobs and low unemployment, while expanding basic services to citizens throughout the country. Between 1945 and 1969 the unemployment rate averaged 4.5% and in 1969 was 3.6%. The GNP rose from $335.2 billion in 1945 to $725.6 billion in 1969; the manufacturing index rose from 75.6 to 189.5. By 1970 telephone service was provided to 90% of households compared to 22% in 1945.[11]

So successful were the largest U.S. firms that foreign governments feared their further expansion and foreign businesses began to pay the ultimate compliment of emulation. As businesses began to recover from the war, firms in nation after nation began to adopt the new decentralized vertically integrated structure common to U.S. corporations.[12] So formidable was the American business expansion abroad that it aroused suspicion and hostile reaction in a number of foreign countries. In this era other nations looked on US management as the model for modern business. There was fear that America's multinationals, using their technological advantages, their modern organizational techniques and their abundant capital would simply squeeze out the significant indigenous producers.[13]

U.S. MANAGEMENT SLOW TO ADAPT TO DEMANDS OF GLOBAL ECONOMY

Economic recovery in Japan and Europe by the early 1970s allowed those countries to compete for a share of the U.S. market. Japanese and European businesses, because of their relatively small domestic markets, had historically focused on international trade as an important source of economic growth.

Rapid growth of international trade during the 1970s was facilitated by the General Agreement on Tariff and Trade (GATT), which improved international financing tools and advanced transportation and communication technologies and globalization of sales and marketing.

The GATT Agreement was signed in 1947. Supported by the U.S., it enhanced international trade by reducing tariffs. International financing provided by the World Bank and U.S., European, and Japanese banks increased capital investment in Europe and Japan. New transportation technologies, including containerization and jet air cargo carriers, reduced the time and cost of transporting goods. Communication technologies, including satellites, improved the quality and timeliness of communication. Growth of large scale retail outlets in the U.S. provided an efficient way to distribute goods. Foreign television manufacturers have gained a sizable share of the U.S. market simply by supplying a dozen large American department store chains.

> In 1980 19% of goods Americans made were exported (up from 9% in 1970) and more than 22% of goods Americans used were imported (up from 9% in 1970). . . . By 1980 more than 70% of all goods produced in the United States were actively competing with foreign-made goods. . . . By 1981 America was importing about 26% of its cars, 25% of its steel, 60% of its televisions, radios, tape recorders and 43% of its calculators, 27% of its metal forming machine tools, 35% of its textile machinery, and 53% of its numerically controlled machine tools. Twenty years before imports had accounted for less than 10% of the U.S. market for each of these products.[14]

Liberal trade policies and other macroeconomic factors may have helped to improve the competitive position of many foreign-based companies. However, micro analysts discount these factors and focus on ineffective U.S. management practices and policies as the reason for declining U.S. competitiveness during this period.

Throughout the 1970s German, Japanese and French governments maintained a larger debt in proportion to their national economies than did the American Government. Investment in Research and Development declined from 3% of the Gross National Product at the start of the 1970s to 2% at the start of the 1980s. But this decline stemmed mostly from a slowdown in public financed defense and space programs which affected American industry only indirectly. U.S. expenditures for research and development was still higher then those of its competitors.[15]

U.S. manufacturing firms at the beginning of the 1970s focused on their domestic market and were members of stable oligopolies that encouraged volume, discouraged competition, and failed to reward innovation. Management practices and policies emphasized financial control in order to manage divisions. Cost and profit centers were created, and performance was based on meeting annual budgets; rewards were given based on immediate bottom-line results. Industrial companies operated primarily under a mechanistic system that focused on narrow job functions. Layers of middle management were created to communicate management goals downward and report results of operation upward. Global strategies were ignored.

These management practices were no longer effective in a competitive global economy driven by the following factors:

1. Increasing fragmentation and volatility of consumer buying patterns that demand the highest quality goods in the shortest possible time;
2. Faster diffusion of the latest advances in science and technology that can transform industries, production methods and product designs in days rather than years;
3. The spawning of new learning organizations from every part of the globe that can design and produce and innovate faster than ever before; and,
4. An enormous propagation in the number of different technologies and skills required for companies to compete across different industries and products. [16]

"Companies now had to compete simultaneously on three fronts: The price of their products, their quality and the product line."[17] These factors required a melding of narrow functional job specifications and the creation of a team approach that required a more democratic and less autocratic management style. It was necessary to develop an organic structure with more open communication between management and workers. The organic structure required fewer management layers and a strong corporate culture with core values that could unify a corporation that employed knowledge, workers, and extended beyond national boundaries. To compete, the corporation would have to transform itself from a national or multinational corporation to a global corporation that would identify itself not as an American entity doing business in foreign countries but a global entity based in the U.S.

Criticism of U.S. management practices and strategies stemmed from management's inability to adapt to the global economy and the success that Japanese and European firms had in penetrating U.S. markets. Management policies and strategies employed by Japanese and European firms were analyzed and praised, notwithstanding the cultural context or the economic environment that made it difficult for U.S. companies to emulate their foreign competitors.

U.S. management practices, in a state of flux, were criticized as managers attempted through trial and error to determine what needed to be changed, how to implement the change, and what practices to implement. During this state of flux, management attempted to maintain profit margins in the face of declining market share. Policies they employed usually provided short-term profits but were harmful in the long-term. The short-term expediency of management was criticized, but the underlying causes were usually not addressed. Critics did not often recognize that the management practices, strategies, and policies employed from 1920 to 1970 had provided unparalleled economic prosperity and U.S. industrial domination. It is difficult to realize that changes in the external environment can make once successful strategies and policies obsolete. It is more difficult to make changes when stability was the rule and the policies that had to be changed were successful for a very long period of time.

FACTORS UNDERLYING STRATEGIES EMPLOYED BY FOREIGN-BASED COMPANIES

Global strategies such as strategic intent[18] core competencies,[19] and megamarketing[20] were used as examples of superior global management strategies employed by foreign-based firms. Quality work circles,[21] TQM,[22] and Deming's quality control procedure [23] were used as examples of superior Japanese management practices that fostered teamwork and employee commitment and produced quality products.

Many theorists argue that the global strategies of Japanese firms are based on and evolve from Japan's history and its economic, political, and social systems. They note that Japan's history over the past 150 years is based on catching up to Western societies in order to protect itself. The Meiji oligarchy took control of Japan in 1868 as a result of the fear, born from the treaty negotiations with the U.S. in 1853, that the western world would soon dominate Japan. The Meiji leaders were obsessed with making Japan a strong nation that could defend itself against external threats. "Industrialization at a furious tempo was taken for granted . . . catching up with the strongest in the world became an obsession."[24]

Industrialization in Japan was born with significant government involvement. The Japanese government directly put up capita to create the national railway, communication networks, and the armament, mining, and shipbuilding industries. In 1880, the government gave away what it had built by privatizing industries it controlled and establishing an economic oligarchy of financial houses, the bureaucratic elite, and those politically privileged, over which it retained significant influence.[25]

The economic oligarchy's objective was and continues to be the development of a modern Western industrial state. To achieve this goal, Japan required access to raw materials and world markets. To gain access to raw materials, Japan during the first half of the twentieth century, used military means which proved a failure. During the second half of the twentieth century, the economic oligarchy is using a quality industrial approach to achieve its objectives.[26]

GLOBAL STRATEGIES USED BY FOREIGN-BASED FIRMS

Strategic Intent

Underlying the concept of strategic intent is the pursual of a goal that is out of all proportion to present resources and capabilities. "Strategic intent is defined as an obsession with winning at all levels and a sustained obsession over the 10-20 year quest for global leadership."[27] Strategic intent implies a sizable stretch for an organization. Current capabilities and resources will not suffice. This situation forces the organization to be more inventive and make the most of limited resources. While the traditional view of strategy focuses on the degree of plausible outcomes based on existing resources and current opportunities, strategic intent creates extremely ambitious, usually implausible outcomes based on the discrepancy between resources and ambition.[28] Attempts to bridge this stretch create a relentless and obsessive drive similar to the obsession of catching up to the West observed during the Meiji period.

The ability to apply the concept of strategic intent requires the support of financial sources and shareholders who see global leadership as a top priority. Financial sources must agree to provide loans that are by Western standards equity financing. Shareholders must agree to forego short-term return on investment for uncertain future returns.

Most large firms in Japan belong to conglomerates known as corporate groups or Keiretsu. These groups are highly diversified industrial companies clustered around their own bank.

> Between 60% and 70% of all shares outstanding on the Japan stock exchange are held by Japanese corporations and financial institutions. They keep these shares within their conglomerate family in a pattern of reciprocal shareholding. Because these shares are considered to be political shares rather than investments they are never sold.[29]

The holding of political shares reduces the pressure to earn immediate profits and facilitates the implementation of strategic intent. In the 1970s the leading companies listed on the first section of the Tokyo Stock Exchange paid on average 1.5%; this represented the lowest payout in the world.[30]

The Central Bank of Japan has allowed firms to borrow up to 80% of their capital from banks they have a Keiretsu relationship with.

> Heavily over-loaned as they were for most of the post war years the banks pumping funds into the Keiretsu became increasingly dependent on the central bank. The dependency allowed the bureaucrats at the central bank and the Ministry of Finance which has influence over the central bank to direct funding of major industries based as national priorities.[31]

In the West, over-leveraging the banking system with equity-based loans to companies stretching their resources in search of strategic intent would cause a banking crisis and several government investigations. U.S. institutional investors tend to reject companies that do not show strong quarterly earnings per share, and U.S. banks will not continue lending to companies that report losses while building market share.

In Japan, confidence in the economic oligarchy—and the relationship between government bureaucrats, politicians, and company executives dating back to the Meiji period—allows for aggressive lending and over leveraging of assets. These factors are necessary for the successful implementation of the concept of strategic intent.

From the concept of strategic intent a global competitive framework was developed. The global competitive framework identified tactics that could be used to build a global presence. Accessing global volume by finding loose bricks, redefining cost volume relationships by investing in technological improvements, and developing franchise brands were tactics used by Japanese and European firms to gain significant global market share in many industrial sectors.[32]

Using the concept of strategic intent, Japan decided to move away from existing industries like radios and textile goods and moved into technology-based businesses such as steel, oil refinery, petrochemicals, and automobiles.[33] As part of this strategy, conglomerate companies evolved using core businesses as a base for diversifying into new emerging areas of opportunity.[34] A small player in the watch industry, Seiko overcame Timex on the low end and Swiss firms on the high end and established a worldwide brand name. From watches, Seiko diverted into personal computer printers, electronic components, batteries, audio equipment, and graphic display systems.

The conglomerate structure underlies this growth and ability to move out of declining industries and quickly into emerging new industries. The conglomerate structure provides size, scope, and financial resources required to enter new industries and to outlive the competition. The Japanese conglomerate is well-managed and has been able to develop tightly integrated structure, culture, and organizational goals that the American conglomerate has not been able to do.[35]

> When asked where he works, a Japanese worker will typically answer, "I belong to Hitachi." Being hired by a large company and being granted lifetime employment bestows considerable prestige and is viewed by typical workers as a vote of confidence which they in turn are expected to justify on an ongoing basis. . . . When people

introduce themselves, they state first the company's name, their last name and their position in the company.[36]

The successful implementation of the tactics and strategies used by foreign corporations to gain global market share requires significant risk capital, a supportive banking system, and patient stockholders. These are factors found in Japan and Europe where a more integrated relationship between government, business, and banks exist. In Germany bank personnel sit on the board of directors of their clients. In the U.S. this would create a potential conflict of interest that could jeopardize a bank's creditor status. In the U.S. environment a mishap in employing a critical strategy can make a company prey to a takeover and the calling of bank loans. In Japan with 60% to 70% of stock held for political purposes, the word "takeover" means hijack.

Megamarketing

The concept of megamarketing broadens the definition of marketing to include influencing government bureaucrats, political leaders, and other opinion makers. This concept has been credited with helping the Japanese to penetrate the U.S. market. Successful megamarketing requires a much higher level of funding than marketing requires.[37] These resources are allocated by the Japanese government and Japanese firms because they help meet a top Japanese national priority.

Core Competency

The strategy of developing core competencies has been identified as a factor that has allowed NEC, Cannon, and Honda to obtain significant global market share in their respective industries.[38] Like strategic intent and megamarketing, this strategy requires the employment of significant resources and a long-term commitment. The establishment of core competencies requires the development of corporate-wide skills that cut across divisional lines and reduces the accountability of cost and profit centers.[39] The Japanese corporation and society, with its emphasis on collective responsibilities, is better suited to adopting this concept than American firms and the American society, which emphasizes individual and business unit responsibility.

Knowledge-, Productivity- and Alliance-Based Strategies

Knowledge, productivity and alliance-based strategies have been identified as the three patterns underlying Japanese global strategies.[40]

The knowledge-based strategy recognizes the importance of high value products in the era of human capital. "The knowledge-based strategy strives for ever higher rates of value added in products (i.e., goods, services and process such as information and design) due to the multiplier of knowledge intensive inputs in proportion to other inputs such as mundane energy, materials and physical labor."[41]

The knowledge-based strategy recognizes the rise of the knowledge worker, the information-based organizations, and the decoupling of labor from production. The strategy also recognizes that the future is not in volume-based production but in precision products, customer products, and technology-driven products.[42]

Productivity-based strategy is described as "continuously moving both capital and human resources to ever higher valued use in production processes (or service delivery systems) in conjunction with minimizing non-productive investments."[43] By employing this strategy, Japanese companies are better able to comply with price, quality, and flexibility pressures of the global marketplace.

The productivity-based strategy is very different from the non-productive paper entrepreneurship employed by U.S. managers. American managers unable to adapt to the knowledge- or productivity-based strategies have sought to increase their firm's profits through accounting, tax avoidance, litigation, and mergers and acquisitions. "Paper entrepreneurship is supplanting product entrepreneurship as the most dynamic and innovative business in the American economy."[44]

"The alliance-based strategy is based on an alliance of workers and stakeholders but not competitors. This means: A. Seeking a mutually trusting self-maintaining relationship, resulting in minimal internal and external investments in coercive control systems, B. which results in win-win arrangements or mutual gains."[45]

The alliance-based strategy is compatible with the ideology of communitarianism found in Japan and other Asian countries and to an extent in many European countries. Under this ideology the community "is more than the sum of the individuals in it; the community is organic not atomistic. It has special and urgent needs as a community. Individual fulfillment derives from a sense of identity, participation and usefulness in a community."[46]

The individualist ideology that dominates American society sees self-fulfillment and self-respect as "realized through an essential lonely struggle. The fit survive; if you do not survive, it is because you are somehow unfit."[47]

Tactics and Other Manufacturing Strategies Employed by Foreign Based Companies

From the knowledge-, productivity-, and alliance-based strategies identified come a series of tactics listed in Table I that have contributed to the success many foreign-based firms have had in increasing global market share. Four evolutionary stages of Japanese manufacturing strategy have been identified which complement the tactics listed in Table 1.[48]

The four stages identified are low labor costs (Stage 1), capital intensive focused factors (Stage 2), flexible factories (Stage 3), and flexible factories with time-based strategies (Stage 4). The flexible factory was developed in the late 1970s and early 1980s as a response to the narrow focus forced on companies that captured specialized markets by producing a greater variety of goods. Factories using flexible and time-based strategies can respond to rapid product development cycles by introducing a greater variety of products in a shorter time.[49]

Foreign-based competition since 1960 has developed proactive global strategies that helped it gain global market share in critical manufacturing industries at the expense of U.S.-based companies. These proactive strategies have helped create market demand much as the Sony Walkman created a market for headphones. Global strategies, including the four evolutionary stages of Japanese manufacturing, core competencies, and strategic intent, created new expectations in terms of price, quality, broad product lines, and timeliness.[50] U.S.-based firms are responding to these market requirements. However, many business and government leaders believe they will not catch up until their strategies are proactive and create new market demands that foreign-based firms will have to respond to.

Global based strategies employed by foreign-based firms can be viewed as resulting from history, culture, and the economic, political, and social systems found in the domicile of the foreign-based firm. These strategies are also viewed as employing basic business principles. David Packard, co-founder of Hewlett-Packard noted,

"There are no secrets to their success. They have simply carried out their business basics very well."[51] Others note,

> Japan's industrial success is the result not of cheating or of culture but of adherence to business basics, and that the Japanese advantage lies not in secret or esoteric knowledge or technique but rather in the practice of what is known. . . . Understanding global competitiveness today lies in strategically applying simple creative forces—ones such as knowledge, alliance and productivity.[52]

U.S. MANAGEMENT SLOW TO ADAPT TO NEEDS OF TODAY'S WORKER

Management practices employed by foreign-based companies are also viewed as critical factors that have allowed for the successful development and implementation of global strategies. These practices have been viewed as either developing from history and culture or adhering to basic management principles.

> Management is about human beings. Its task is to make people capable of joint performances, to make their strengths effective and their weaknesses irrelevant. . . . This is what organization is all about and it is the reason that management is the critical determining factor. . . . Because management deals with the integration of people in a common venture, it is deeply embedded in culture.[53]

"Knowledge workers are fast becoming the pace setters in societies of all developed countries."[54] Knowledge workers are specialists who are aware that they have more knowledge in their field than their manager or employer. "The knowledge worker is a colleague and an associate rather than a subordinate; he has to be managed as such"[55] The knowledge worker is more autonomous, less fearful of punishment, and is motivated by a higher order of needs. Managers must learn to work with knowledge workers because "even when they are not a majority in their organization, they increasingly set the norms and the standards."[56]

Frederick Taylor's Scientific Management theory and the Autocratic Management style have been the basis of worker management relations in the U.S. since the early 1900s. The Autocratic or Theory X management style was encouraged by labor unions in the post World War II years. Even when favorable wage settlements were negotiated, unions advocated an adversarial relationship between management and workers because it created union loyalty among workers. Even among non-union workers, this adversarial relationship existed. Management did little to improve their relationship with workers, believing that higher pay and benefit packages in union and non-union contracts were the only tools available to motivate workers and create loyalty.

FACTORS UNDERLYING MANAGEMENT PRACTICES EMPLOYED BY FOREIGN-BASED COMPANIES

History and Culture

Throughout the 1960s while union contracts in major industrial sectors brought increased pay and benefits, worker absenteeism increased and workmanship declined. On Monday and Friday absenteeism at many GM plants was 20%. which even union officers did not understand. Drug use and rowdiness in plants increased substantially and so did product rejects and defects. Productivity growth stagnated. American managers looked for answers in Japan and Europe.

> Japanese management operated with weak unions and a submissive middle class of salarymen. Except for seamen, teachers and groups of public workers whose nationwide unions could not be clearly tamed there are today only management supported company unions which more often than not actively participate in campaigns to maximize production at the cost of worker comfort. . . . Thus there is no conflict between management and organized workers.[57]

The corporate fast track invariably includes a stint working full time for the company union and the company board of directors generally includes former union leaders . . . all this is conducive to flexible management.[58]

Underlying the behavior of the salaryman, originally named for the salary he received as distinct from wages of factory hands and others lower in the occupational hierarchy, is Japanese history and culture that dictates:

1. That work units and not families are the basic building blocks of Japanese society.[59]
2. Japanese loyalty is directed solely at a group or person not a belief or abstract idea.[60]
3. The bond between company and employee can only be maintained so long as the employee has nowhere else to hire out his services. In most cases he hasn't.[61]
4. The salaryman goes through an education system whose function is to shape a generation of disciplined workers for techno-mechanic systems that require highly socialized individuals capable of performing reliably in a hierarchical and finely tuned organization environment.[62]

It is under the Japanese culture and economic system that the company union, a submissive salaryman class, a communitarian ideology, and an economic oligarchy is maintained. It is from these ideals that collective responsibility, a commitment to long-term employment, and long-term planning horizons have become the basis of Japanese management practices.

Collective Responsibility: Long-Term Employment

Collective responsibility allows for successful implementation of Japanese management practices that focus on consensus decision making and participatory management. It also enables the successful implementation of quality circles and total quality management techniques and advanced manufacturing processes. Commitment to long-term employment allows management to invest in employee training and development, which encourages non-specialized career paths, reduces turnover, and increases loyalty. Korean corporations, which operate under a culture that values a collective approach, have been able to emulate Japanese management practices. "Samsung exhibits the mixture of Theory A and Theory J in such a way that it may be called a living Theory Z organization."[63]

Transplanting Japanese management practices onto firms run by U.S. managers has been difficult because of the individualistic ideology that dominates American culture. It is difficult for U.S. companies to implement many Japanese management practices that were in fact developed in the U.S. "The use of the Japanese management practice of participative management has had only mixed results in the U.S. and has sometimes been a divisive instead of a cohesive force between workers and supervisors."[64]

American managers adhere to an individualist ideology that does not encourage participatory and consensus management practices. In 1989 U.S. chief executives were paid twice the amount that German, French and British chief executives were paid and three times the amount of the average Japanese chief executive. At the largest Japanese companies, top executives earn about seventeen times more than the average worker while in the U.S., the multiplier is 109.[65]

> The U.S. manager grows up to think he and his personal interests come first. His goals then are to maximize his own wealth and to increase his individual power and glory. . . . Young managers are taught to watch out for Number 1 and get on the fast track, negotiate fat benefit packages and golden parachutes and move every three years in order to maximize rapid promotion. Loyalty to a company or to one's colleagues is considered outmoded and rarely practiced.[66]

Golden parachutes and salary increases to executives, in the face of layoffs, losses, and reduced market shares, do not lead to consensus and participatory management. "When Mazda Motor Corporation of Japan was warned by the transportation ministry to pay strict attention to the safety of its cars in connection with a recall of 3,500 vehicles, Chairman Kericho Yamoto and 17 other top executives immediately took a 10% pay cut."[67]

It is noted that Japanese management practices have often been successful when applied by Japanese firms and managers in American factories. "When Sanyo Manufacturing Company took over a nearly bankrupt television set manufacturing plant in Arkansas in 1977, it was already unionized. By 1982 the use of Japanese management practices changed the workforce from 500 dispirited workers to 2,200 highly motivated employees."[68] "An example of Japanese commitment to training in America took place at Nissan's truck manufacturing plant in Tennessee. Out of a total capital expenditure of $500 million, $56 million was spent on training with almost $30 million of that for training of technicians alone."[69]

It appears that management practices based on long planning horizons, commitment to long-term employment, and collective responsibility are being well-received by U.S. workers. These practices appear to meet the needs of knowledge workers and encourages joint performance, flexibility, and improved efficiency and quality. Many analysts of the global economy note that U.S.-based industries will have difficulty competing with foreign competitors unless their executives modify their behavior.[70]

MANUFACTURING CONCEPTS THAT MEET DEMANDS OF GLOBAL MARKETPLACE

Manufacturing concepts that must be implemented to compete in the global economy include Just In Time Management Control, Zero Deficits, Design for Manufacturing and Assembly (DFMA), Computer Integrated Manufacturing, and Flexible Manufacturing. These manufacturing concepts require management practices that encourage trust and interdependence, participatory management, teamwork, cooperation, and long-term horizons.

Efficiencies are increased by Just in Time Management (JIT) because set-up costs and economic lot size are reduced. Just In Time Management involves a system of repetitive, lotless manufacturing. Parts and subassemblies are completed "just in time" to go on to the next process.[71] "JIT provides a smooth flow of work through the plant but it has to be associated with total quality control."[72]

An absence of crisis management in the plant and excellent equipment maintenance and teamwork on the factory floor are factors that help facilitate the implementation of the concept of zero defects in Japan.[73]

> Design for Manufacturing and Assembly (DFMA) is a comprehensive strategy for managing ideas to market. . . . It used a cross-functional team approach. . . . DFMA has reduced new product introduction time by 50%-75%. Working on new product development from the outset a team represents all functions that have an impact on both development and introduction and may include representatives from marketing, product development and manufacturing and possibly from the legal sector, safety, product liability and the consumer base. . . . Time-based innovative strategies like DFMA have cut new car development at Honda from five to three years, have cut phone development at AT&T from two to one year and cut truck development at Navistar from five to two and a half years.[74]

Computer Integrated Manufacturing (CIM) brings the latest advances in telecommunication, computers and materials handling techniques into the factory. By linking up SMART multi-mission tools with computerized inventory controls in one integrated platform, CIM offered unparalleled flexibility to produce a growing variety of different product configurations. . . . CIM-based factories thrive under conditions of multiple product designs, small batch orders, decentralized authority and fast turnaround.[75]

Teamwork and collective responsibility are elements that allow CIM to be successful. Flexible Manufacturing meets the demands of the global marketplace by emphasizing shorter product runs that create a variety of products at the price of producing one. Non-specialized career paths and generalist classifications within factories are based on long-term commitment to employees and collective responsibility. The generalist classification gives companies increased flexibility to deploy workers. The outgrowth of the generalized classification is the self-managed work teams which facilitate the implementation of the Flexible Manufacturing process. The self-managed team requires workers to make decisions they have not had to make In the past. The teams schedule themselves, move members from task to task to meet demands, and accept responsibility for quality and intergroup coordination.[76]

RECIPES FOR FIRM COMPETITIVENESS

Recipes for firm competitiveness in the global economy identify teamwork, low turnover, and long-term planning horizons as key factors. For example, thirty-nine of Germany's most successful exporters listed the following five common practices as critical for competing successfully in the global economy:

1. Combine strategic factors with geographic diversity.
2. Blend technology and closeness to customers.
3. Emphasize factors like customer value.
4. Rely on their own technical competence.
5. Create mutual interdependence between the company and its employees.[77]

A second recipe, lists five imperatives that are necessary to make an enterprise competitive:

1. Leverage internal resources to meet the changing needs of a marketplace by distributing real decision-making power to the people who are close to the answer.
2. Responsiveness to customers.
3. Flexibility in manufacturing.
4. Empowerment of technology-savvy managers.
5. Reliance on alliances and partnerships, particularly between buyer and vendor.[78]

William Glavin President of Babson College and former Vice Chairman of Xerox Corporation provides a third recipe when he notes,

We are going to have multiple countries competing for the same business. Fulfilling customer requirements with lower costs will be the driving factor in successes. And the people who spend the time looking at how to do things differently, more cost effectively, and right the first time are more likely to succeed.[79]

To succeed, P. Ranganoth Nayak, Senior Vice President at Arthur D. Little, notes that a manager must husband three kinds of capital simultaneously. "One is finance, which is the traditional thing we have thought about; one is the attitude of your customers towards you and their satisfaction with what you do; and the third is the dedication of your employees."[80] The three forms of capital interact and are interdependent. Dedicated employees and financial capital facilitate the implementation of manufacturing processes that allow firms to satisfy customers.

CONCLUSION

Micro proponents look at the successful implementation of global strategies and management practices employed by foreign-based firms as the reason why these firms have become dominant in markets that were once controlled by U.S.-based industries. Initially, U.S.-based companies did not counter foreign competitive strategies because they did not recognize the threat they posed. This complacency, born from fifty years of economic stability and prosperity, was achieved in part by oligopolies in major manufacturing sectors that discouraged innovation and encouraged management practices that emphasized individual responsibility, short-term employment, and short-term planning.

Underlying the global strategies of foreign-based competitors is an economic, political and social system, as well as a culture and history that support long-term planning, collective responsibility, and long-term employment. Foreign firms were able to successfully implement their strategies because they were able to obtain equity based loans and capital that did not demand immediate payback. Foreign firms were also able to develop management practices from within and emulate management practices of others that conformed to their culture and history. These management practices and global strategies created increased customer expectations and demands by creating manufacturing processes that produced customized innovative product lines quickly.

Micro proponents focus on global strategies of foreign competitors, their management practices, ideology, culture, or adherence to basic business principles as the basis of competitive advantage. At the same time, U.S. management has been criticized for short-term thinking, ineffective autocratic management practices, being greedy and looking out for No. 1 only. American workers have also been criticized for lack of loyalty and a reduced work ethic. Micro proponents believe that U.S. firms must become competitive at the firm level.

> Domestic interests might not always run parallel with the compulsion of the corporation to survive in a global marketplace. This may bring us into conflict with our nation or so it may seem at first. At the end the benefit of the corporation will coincide with that of the nation. No American gains if our corporations perish.[81]

NOTES

1. Peter Buckley, C.L. Pass and Kate Prescott, "Foreign Market Servicing Strategies and Competitiveness", *Journal of General Management*, Winter 1991, 34.

2. Michael T. Jacobs, *Short Term America*, 4.

3. Louis Galambos and Joseph Pratt, *The Rise of the Corporate Commonwealth*, 74.

4. Ibid., 90.

5. Ibid., 161.

6. Ibid., 160.

7. Ibid., 160.

8. Robert Reich, *The Next American Frontier*, 48.

9. Ibid., 49-50.

10. Ibid., 50.

11. Louis Galambos and Joseph Pratt, *The Rise of the Corporate Commonwealth*, 181-182.

12. Ibid., 182.

13. Ibid., 169-170.

14. Robert Reich, *The Next American Frontier*, 121-122.

15. Ibid., 120-121.

16. Joel D. Goldhar and David Lei, "The Shape of Twenty-First Century Global Manufacturing," *The Journal of Business Strategy*, March/April 1991, 58.

17. P.T. Bolwijn and T. Kumpe, "Manufacturing in the 1990s - Productivity, Flexibility and Innovation," *Long Range Planning*, August 1990, 46.

18. Gary Hamel and C.K. Prahalad, "Strategic Intent" 17-30.

19. C.K. Prahalad and Gary Hamel, "Core Competence of the Corporation", 79-91.

20. Philip Kotler, *Megamarketing*, 117-124.

21. G. Munchus III, "Employer-Employee Based Quality Circles in Japan: Human Resource Policy Implications for American Firms", *Academy of Management Review*, 1983, 255-26 1.

22. John Scally, "Actions Speak Louder then Buzzwords," *National Productivity Review*, Autumn 1993, 453-456.

23. Yoshida Kosaku, "Deming's Management Philosophy: Does It Work in the U.S. as Well as in Japan," *The Columbia Journal of World Business*, Fall 1989, 10-17.

24. Karel Van Wolferen, *The Enigma of Japanese Power*, 376, (New York: Random House, 1989), 376.

25. Ibid., 377.

26. Ken Getterman, "No Change, but Relentless Change," *Modern Machine Shop*, March 1991, 94.

27. Hamel and Prahalad, "Strategic Intent," 18.

28. Ibid., 18.

29. Wolferen, *The Enigma of Japanese Power*, 46.

30. Ibid., 396.

31. Ibid., 385.

32. Hamel and Prahalad, "Strategic Intent," 23-25.

33. Milton Leontiades, "The Japanese Art of Managing Diversity," *The Journal of Business Strategy*, March-April 1991,30

34. Ibid, 31.

35. Ibid., 35.

36. David Aviel, "Why the United States Isn't Winning the Trade War with Japan," *IM*, March/April 1990, 14.

37. Philip Kotler, "Megamarketing", 127.

38. Prahalad and Hamel, "Core Competence of the Corporation," 87.

39. Ibid., 86.

40. Norman P. Smothers, "Patterns of Japanese Strategy; Strategic Combinations of Strategies," *Strategic Management Journal*, April 1990, 521.

41. Ibid., 523.

42. Robert Reich, *The Next American Frontier*, 128-129.

43. Norman P. Smothers, " Patterns of Japanese Strategy," 521.

44. Robert Reich, *The Next American Frontier*, 157.

45. Norman P. Smothers, "Patterns of Japanese Strategy," 523.

46. George C. Lodge, *The American Disease*, (New York: Alfred A Knopf, 1984), 44-45.

47. Ibid., 40.

48. George Stalk Jr. "Time—The Next Source of Competitive Advantage," *Harvard Business Review*, July/August 1988, 41.

49. Ibid., 43.

50. P.T Bolwijn and T. Kumpe, "Manufacturing in the 1990s," 45.

51. Norman P. Smothers, "Patterns of Japanese Strategy," 532

52. Ibid., 532.

53. Peter Drucker, *The New Realities*, 229.

54. Ibid., 187.

55. Ibid., 180.

56. Ibid., 186.

57. Karel Van Wolferen, *The Enigma of Japanese Power*, 167.

58. David Hamel, "DMF Easy if You Know How." *Machine Design*, January 8, 1993, 27.

59. Karel Van Wolferen, *The Enigma of Japanese Power*, 167.

60. Ibid., 169.

61. Ibid., 162.

62. Ibid., 83.

63. Mushin Lee, "Samsung uses Theory Z to Become a Living Organization," *IM*, September/October 1992, 30.

64. Ronald Sheldon and Brian Kleiner, "What Japanese Management Techniques Can (or Should) be Applied by American Managers," *IM*, May/June 1990, 19.

65. Michael T. Jacobs, *Short Term America*, 202.

66. David Aviel, "Why the United States Isn't Winning the Trade War with Japan," *IM*, March/April 1990, 15.

67. Michael T. Jacobs, *Short Term America*, 27.

68. Ronald Sheldon and Brian Kleiner, "What Japanese Management Techniques Can (or Should) be Applied by American Managers," 18.

69. Ibid., 18.

70. Ibid., 19.

71. Ibid., 19.

72. O.P. Kharbanda, "Japan's Lessons for the West," *CMA Magazine*, February 1992, 29.

73. Ronald Sheldon, and Brian Kleiner, "What Japanese Management Techniques Can (or Should by Applied by American Managers," 19.

74. W. Christopher Musselwhite, "Time Based Innovation: The New Competitive Advantage," *Training and Development Journal*, January 1990, 54-55.

75. Joel Goldhar and David Lei, "The Shape of Twenty-First Century Global Manufacturing," *The Journal of Business Strategy*, March/April 1991, 58.

76. William Nowlin, "Restructuring In Manufacturing Management, Work and Labor Relations," *IM*, November/December 1990, 7.

77. Herman Simon, "Lessons from Germany's Midsize Giants," *Harvard Business Review*, March/April 1992, 116.

78. "The Path to the Globally Competitive Enterprise," *Modern Material Handling*, April 1990, 78.

79. John S. McClennhen, "Can You Manage in the New Economy," *Industry Week*, 27.

80. Ibid., 26.

81. "Japan: Should We Copy to Compete?," *Automation*, 61.

CHAPTER 5

Identifying Competitive U.S.-Based Industries and Companies

Chapters 2 through 4 indicate that research to date has been primarily focused either on broad-based, ineffective public policy or ineffective management strategies and practices as the cause of a decline in U.S. industrial competitiveness. The heterogeneity of U.S. industry may make this approach inappropriate when trying to ascertain the factors that determine competitiveness. This book looks at the *industry* level to determine which industries lost, maintained, or improved their competitive position during the period 1981-1992. When an industry was found to have improved its competitive position despite the overall trend, it was further examined in an attempt to determine the factors that led to improvements in its competitiveness. Only manufacturing industries were studied because of the dominance of manufacturing trade.

INCREASING IMPORTANCE OF MANUFACTURING TRADE

Table 5-1 shows that manufacturing trade, defined as commodities included in SITC categories 5-8, increased its total percentage of world trade from 57.4% in 1981 to 70.5% in 1987 and 74.1% in 1991. Table 5-2 indicates that the average annual growth rate for manufactured trade was greater than all other commodities for the periods 1980-1991, 1980-1988 and 1988-1991. The high percentage of total trade for SITC 3 in 1981, reflected in Table 5-1, is due to the oil crisis. A decline in the percentage of world trade and the growth rate of SITC 3 after 1981 shown in Tables 5-1 & 5-2 reflects a resolution of the oil crises.

"Improvements in the Merchandise Trade Balance must come primarily from the manufactures trade account; the other components of merchandise trade do not offer the potential for major improvements."[1]

In a world where most goods are readily tradable and most services are not, the manufacturing sector is the primary interface of the U.S. economy with the world economy; it is the sector most exposed to foreign competition.[2]

DATA GATHERING

Data in U.S. exports and imports for all 3-digit SITC codes within manufacturing categories 5-8 have been compiled using the United Nations International Trade Statistics Yearbooks for the years 1980-1992 to determine the dollar value, market share and numerical ranking of exports and imports.

The National Trade Data Base has been used to convert competitive 3-digit SITC codes to 4-digit SIC codes. Utilizing the 1993 Wards Business Directory, companies within competitive 4-digit SIC coded industries have been identified. Finally, secondary sources, including trade and business journals, have been utilized to determine the factors that make these companies competitive.

Table 5-1
Structure of World Exports by Commodity Class

SITC		1975	1981	1987	1990	1991
		%	%	%	%	%
	All Commodities SITC	100.0	100.0	100.0	100.0	100.0
0 & 1	Food, Live Animals, Beverages, Tobacco	11.9	10.2	9.1	8.7	8.9

Table 5-1 continued

2 & 4	Crude Materials Oil & Fats (Fuels excluded)	7.5	6.6	5.7	5.2	4.7
3	Minerals, Fuels, Lubricants, Related Materials	19.4	24.1 [1]	11.3	10.1	9.5
5	Chemicals	7.0	7.3	8.7	8.8	8.7
7	Machinery & Transportation Equipment	28.0	26.7	34.3	35.7	36.5
6 & 8	Other Manufactured Goods	24.4	23.4	27.5	28.6	28.9
		98.2	98.3	96.6	97.1	97.2
5, 7, 6 & 8		59.4	57.4	70.5	73.1	74.1

[1]*Oil crisis increased oil prices increasing percentage of SITC category 3.*

Source: 1991 International Trade Statistics Yearbook Volume 1, (New York: United Nations Publishing, 1993), Special Table D 592.

Source: 1992 International Trade Statistics Yearbook Volume 1, (New York: United Nations Publishing, 1993), Special Table D 592.

Table 5-2
Annual Average Growth of Exports by Commodity Class

		1980-1988	1988-1991	1980-1991
SITC		%	%	%
	Total All Commodities	5.0	6.8	5.6
0 & 1	Food, Live Animals, Beverages, Tobacco	3.4	6.3	4.3

Table 5-2 continued

2 & 4	Crude Materials Oil & Fats (Fuels excluded)	2.8	-0.09	1.7
3	Minerals, Fuels, Lubricants, Related Materials	-8.3	7.3	-3.8
5	Chemicals	8.8	5.8	7.9
7	Machinery & Transportation Equipment	9.8	8.3	9.4
6 & 8	Other Manufactured Goods	7.3	8.0	7.5

Source: 1992 International Trade Statistics Yearbook Volume 1, (New York: United Nations Publishing, 1993), Special Table C 588.

DATA ANALYSIS

Tables 5-3 and 5-5 identify the 3-digit SITC coded industries that report dollar value export growth in excess of dollar value import growth and positive export market share growth for the periods 1981-1992, 1981-1987 and 1987-1992. These tables also note the export ranking of these industries and whether they have a positive or negative trade balance at the end of the period analyzed. The 3-digit SITC codes that were deemed to be competitive for the periods analyzed have been identified. Such industries meet the following criteria:

1. Dollar value export growth in excess of import growth.
2. Export market share growth.
3. Export market share growth in excess of import market share growth.
4. Positive trade balance at end of period analyzed.
5. U.S. export ranking in top 10.

Much of the information gathered concerning domestic industries is maintained by SIC classification. To identify firms within U.S. industries that have been identified as competitive (Tables 5-6 and 5-8) during the periods 1981-1992, 1981-1987, and 1987-1992, the data has been converted from 3-digit SITC codes to 4-digit SIC codes using the conversion program produced by the National Trade Data Bank. Industries identified have been cross-referenced to all SITC codes, and those that were not identified as competitive were eliminated.

Those that were identified as competitive are then classified by periods 1981-1992, 1981-1982 and 1987-1992. The major 2-digit SIC categories that had the greatest percentage of competitive 4-digit SIC codes relative to the total possible 4-digit SIC codes within each category were then identified and selected for further study. Using the 1993 Ward Directory the three largest companies (by sales) each 4-digit SIC coded industry was identified for further study.

STATISTICAL FINDINGS

The empirical findings of the study indicate that a significant improvement occurred in U.S. industrial competitiveness during the period 1987-1992 compared to the period 1981-1987. For the period 1981-1987 no 3-digit SITC category met all five criteria while for the period 1987-1992, forty-four 3-digit SITC categories met all five criteria. Where the competitive 3-digit SITC categories were converted to 4-digit SIC codes using a conversion table provided by the National Trade Data Bank, the three largest companies (by sales) within each converted 4-digit SIC codes were also competitive. Competitive companies as a whole developed organic organizational structures, participatory management styles, global corporate strategies and made innovation part of their corporate culture.

Table 5-3 reports that twenty-two 3-digit SITC categories had dollar value export growth greater than import growth and positive export market share growth for the period 1981-1992. Fourteen of the twenty-two categories identified report positive trade balances in 1992. Twelve of the fourteen categories were ranked either 1, 2 or 3 in world exports; one was ranked 4th and one 7th.

Table 5-3
3-Digit SITC Codes with (1) Dollar Value Export Growth in Excess of Import Growth (2) Positive Export Market Share Growth 1981-1992

3-Digit SITC #	Dollar Value Export Growth in Excess of Import Growth	Positive Export Market Share Growth	+ Positive – Negative Trade Balance	Export Ranking
514	41.4	0.7	+	2
533	513.9	2.8	+	2
553	37.0	0.1	+	4
554	309.2	0.2	+	3
572	532.2	1.7	–	1
582	1406.6	6.1	+	2
584	171.8	13.2	+	1
621	87.2	3.4	+	2
655	45.4	1.4	+	7
673	660.8	0.2	–	12
678	3807.6	0.4	–	5
682	407.1	0.9	–	7
685	5.5	2.8	–	8
718	97.4	3.7	+	3
773	719.3	4.7	–	1
781	18537.7	0.3	–	4
785	979.3	4.9	–	4
786	183.4	2.6	+	3
871	239.9	11.1	+	2
872	1155.0	3.3	+	1
892	1271.6	1.8	+	1
898	1600.0	2.4	+	1

Table 5-4 reports that only three 3-digit SITC categories had positive export market share growth and dollar value export growth greater than import growth for the period 1981-1987. One of the three categories identified had positive trade balances in 1987, and for that category the U.S. was ranked as the Number 1 exporter.

Table 5-4
3-Digit SITC Codes with (1) Dollar Value Export Growth in Excess of Import Growth (2) Positive Export Market Share Growth 1981-1987

3-Digit SITC#	Dollar Value Export Growth in Excess of Import Growth	Positive Export Market Share Growth	+ Positive – Negative Trade Balance	Export Ranking
583	125.3	0.4	+	1
785	449.1	0.6	–	5
871	77.4	3.9	–	3

Table 5-5 reports that ninety-two 3-digit SITC categories had dollar value export growth in excess of import growth and positive export market share growth for the period 1987-1992. Forty-eight of the ninety-two categories reported positive trade balances in 1992. Of the forty-eight categories identified, the U.S. was ranked in the top ten of world exporters in all categories.

Table 5-5
3-Digit SITC Codes with (1) Dollar Value Export Growth in Excess of Import Growth
(2) Positive Export Market Share Growth 1987-1992

3-Digit SITC #	Dollar Value Export Growth in Excess of Import Growth	Positive Export Market Share Growth	+ Positive – Negative Trade Balance	Export Ranking
511	400.6	0.9	+	2
512	140.8	1.8	+	2
514	72.8	4.4	+	2
522	314.7	2.8	–	2

Table 5-5 continued

523	12.4	0.2	+	2
524	294.9	9.2	+	2
533	741.8	5.7	+	2
551	195.0	1.0	+	2
553	364.6	4.4	+	4
554	423.3	2.8	+	3
572	4.9	10.8	−	1
582	1440.6	8.5	+	2
583	1334.8	2.3	+	2
584	191.2	16.5	+	1
598	1479.6	3.9	+	2
611	265.7	1.5	+	3
621	50.6	4.5	+	2
625	684.2	3.7	−	4
634	262.0	1.7	−	2
635	282.4	3.6	−	1
641	1554.8	2.3	−	5
642	955.9	3.7	+	2
651	219.5	1.8	+	9
652	101.4	0.9	−	8
655	264.8	3.8	+	7
656	17.9	0.6	−	6
657	486.1	1.9	+	2
659	499.5	4.4	−	2
661	474.4	0.7	−	14
662	43.3	0.4	−	6
663	103.9	0.7	+	3
664	640.6	4.5	+	2
665	93.6	2.7	−	4
674	1203.7	1.8	−	10
676	40.5	0.3	−	8
677	74.2	1.3	−	10
678	1075.2	4.0	−	5
679	42.8	4.5	+	3
682	767.4	2.4	−	7
684	1799.9	4.2	+	2
685	69.0	4.1	−	8

Table 5-5 continued

687	121.3	5.2	–	6
691	367.3	0.8	+	7
692	347.9	4.4	+	2
693	195.7	4.5	–	6
694	282.8	6.0	–	3
695	241.2	3.3	–	3
696	61.6	3.7	+	6
699	1159.4	3.1	–	2
711	129.2	3.5	+	2
712	197.0	5.5	+	3
716	461.6	5.0	+	3
721	904.2	8.3	+	1
722	201.7	6.0	–	2
723	3791.8	11.9	+	1
725	153.8	2.5	–	2
726	418.7	1.4	–	3
727	122.2	2.2	+	3
728	1730.0	0.7	+	4
736	1014.9	4.1	–	3
737	175.6	1.5	+	3
741	1577.7	2.2	+	2
742	441.0	1.9	+	2
743	1983.8	5.3	+	2
744	1666.3	5.8	+	2
745	821.2	4.6	+	3
751	13.0	3.0	–	4
752	7291.4	2.9	–	4
771	454.3	5.2	–	3
773	313.0	2.8	–	1
775	350.4	3.5	–	4
776	716.7	0.9	+	2
778	1663.5	2.8	–	3
781	9394.6	1.9	–	4
782	567.6	0.6	–	4
784	3314.4	2.6	+	2
785	348.2	4.3	–	4
786	348.2	6.2	+	3

Table 5-5 continued

791	158.1	2.6	–	3
793	1060.8	1.4	+	6
821	1109.1	5.1	–	3
846	1342.2	3.2	–	3
871	222.5	7.2	+	2
872	1305.4	10.0	+	1
873	82.4	2.2	–	4
874	2439.0	3.1	+	1
884	37.4	0.8	–	4
885	525.8	0.4	–	8
892	11940.0	6.3	+	1
893	403.7	3.1	–	2
898	2959.5	9.3	+	1
899	326.4	5.1	–	1

Table 5-6 shows that of the fourteen 3-digit SITC categories identified in Table 5-3, eight reported export market share growth in excess of import market share growth for the period 1981-1992. Of the eight categories identified, three are in SITC category 5, one in category 6, and seven and three in category 8.

Table 5-6
Competitive 3-Digit SITC Coded Industries for Period 1981-1992

    1. Dollar Value Export Growth over Import Growth.
    2. Export Market Share Growth.
    3. Export Market Share Growth in Excess of Import Market Share Growth.
    4. Positive Trade Balance 1992.
    5. U.S. Export Ranking in Top Ten 1981-1992.

SITC #	(1)	(2)	(3)
533	513.9	2.8	0.4
582	1406.6	6.1	4.5
584	171.8	13.2	12.6
621	87.8	3.4	0.8
718	97.4	3.7	3.3

Table 5-6 continued

871	239.9	11.1	11.0
892	1271.6	1.8	0.9
898	1600.0	2.4	2.3

It is noted that the one category that met the competitive criteria in Table 5-4 (SITC 5831) did not have export market share growth greater than import market share growth for the period 1981-1987. Table 5-7 shows that the other two SITC categories shown in Table 5-4 (SITC 785 and 871) that met the competitive criteria, except for a negative trade balance in 1987, did have export market share growth in excess of import market share growth. One SITC identified code was in category 7, and one was in category 8.

Table 5-7
Competitive 3-Digit SITC Coded Industries for Period 1981-1987

1. Dollar Value Export Growth over Import Growth.
2. Export Market Share Growth.
3. Export Market Share Growth in Excess of Import Market Share Growth.
4. Positive Trade Balance 1987.
5. U.S. Export Ranking in Top 10 1981-1987.

SITC #	(1)	(2)	(3)
785 (A)	449.1	0.6	8.6
871 (B)	17.4	3.9	3.9

(A) Negative Trade Balance in 1992 <1216.3>
(B) Negative Trade Balance in 1992 <65.27>

Table 5-8 shows that of the forty-eight 3-digit SITC categories identified in Table 5-5, forty-four 3-digit SITC categories reported export market share growth in excess of import market share growth for the period 1987-1992. Of the forty-four categories identified, eleven are in category 5, eleven in category 6, seventeen in category 7, and five in category.8

Table 5-8

Competitive 3-Digit SITC Coded Industries for Period 1987-1992

1. Dollar Value Export Growth over Import Growth.
2. Export Market Share Growth.
3. Export Market Share Growth in Excess of Import Market Share Growth.
4. Positive Trade Balance 1992.
5. U.S. Export Ranking in Top Ten 1987-1992.

SITC #	(1)	(2)	(3)
511	400.6	0.9	2.8
512	140.8	1.8	2.1
523	12.4	0.2	0.1
533	741.8	5.7	5.5
551	195.0	1.0	4.3
553	364.6	4.4	4.1
554	423.3	2.8	3.6
582	1440.6	8.5	7.7
583	1334.8	2.3	0.6
584	191.2	16.5	15.5
598	1479.2	13.9	2.0
611	265.7	1.5	3.3
642	955.9	3.7	6.7
651	219.5	1.8	1.3
655	264.8	3.8	2.9
657	486.1	1.9	4.0
663	103.9	0.7	1.2
664	640.6	4.5	7.4
684	1799.9	4.2	9.0
691	367.3	0.8	4.3
692	347.9	4.4	6.1
696	61.6	3.7	10.2
711	129.2	3.5	5.6
712	197.0	5.5	7.7
716	461.6	5.0	5.4
721	904.2	8.3	10.9
723	122.2	11.9	19.3
727	3791.8	2.2	1.8
728	1730.0	0.7	3.9

Table 5-8 continued

737	175.6	1.5	2.3
741	1577.7	2.2	3.9
742	441.0	1.9	2.0
743	1983.8	5.3	9.8
744	1666.3	5.8	9.3
745	821.2	4.6	6.1
776	716.7	0.9	0.3
784	3314.4	2.6	5.5
786	348.2	6.2	3.7
793	1060.8	1.4	5.0
871	222.5	7.2	7.1
872	1305.4	10.0	8.8
874	2439.0	3.1	2.6
892	11940.0	6.3	8.9
898	2959.5	9.3	1.2

Table 5-6 shows that several industries, despite the overall trend, were competitive during the period 1981-1992. Tables 5-7 and 5-8 indicate that there is a significant improvement in the trade balance of U.S. industries for the period 1987-1992 compared to the period 1981-1987.

Tables 5-9 through 5-12 are classified by SITC categories 5-8. These tables show the conversion of the 3-digit SITC codes to 4-digit SIC codes as follows: the eight competitive 3-digit SITC categories identified in Table 5-6, the two competitive 3-digit SITC categories identified in Table 5-7, and the forty-four competitive 3-digit SITC categories in Table 5-8. After eliminating SIC codes that cross reference to SITC codes not identified in Tables 5-6 through 5-8 (See Tables 5-13 through 5-15), it was found that the remaining SIC codes identified by period in Tables 5-16 through 5-18 were similar.

The SIC codes identified in Table 5-16 as competitive for the period 1981-1992 are also found [except for SIC code 3052 and 3951 in Table 5-18, which identifies competitive SIC codes for the period 1987-1992. The only SIC code identified as competitive 3826 for the period 1981-1987 (Table 5-17), is also found in Table 5-18. Because of the similarity of SIC codes between the periods studied, the competitive

2-digit SIC categories identified in Tables 5-16 through 5-18 and the 4-digit SIC codes within them were grouped and listed in Table 5-19.

Table 5-19 shows that major SIC codes 26, 27, 30, 32, 35, 37, and 38, had the highest percentage of competitive 4-digit codes studied. The 4-digit SIC codes within these major categories were selected for further study. It is noted that the 2-digit SIC group 38 is identified as competitive in all three periods, and 2-digit SIC groups 26, 27 and 30 are identified as competitive in the periods 1981-1992 and 1987-1992. It is further noted that 60% of the 4-digit SIC codes 16 of 10, identified as competitive for the period 1981-1992 have been selected for further study, and the one 4-digit SIC code identified as competitive for the period 1981-1987 has also been selected for further study. Forty-seven of seventy-seven, or 61% of the competitive 4-digit SIC codes for the period 1987-1992, were included for further study.

The industry categories selected for further study include Paper and Allied Products (SlC 26), Printing and Publishing (SIC 27), Rubber and Miscellaneous Plastic Products (SIC 30), Stone Clay and Glass Products (SIC 32), Industrial Machinery and Equipment (SIC 35), Transportation Equipment (SIC 37), and Instruments and Related Products (SIC 38).

Tables 5-20 through 5-26, categorized by the major 2-digit SIC groups selected for further study, identifies the three largest companies (by sales) for each competitive 4-digit SIC code within these 2-digit groups. The author focussed on the management practices and strategies used by the companies identified in Tables 5-20 through 5-26 in an attempt to determine the factors that have made them competitive.

Table 5-9
SITC #5
Conversion of 3-Digit SITC Numbers Identified as Competitive in Tables 5-6 to 5-8 to 4-Digit SIC Codes

3-Digit SITC #	Description	4-Digit SIC #
511	Hydro Carbon	2911
		2865
		2869
512	Alcohols, Phenols	2869

Table 5-9 continued

		2865
		2085
523	Other Inorganic Chemicals	2819
		2874
		2873
		2812
533	Pigments, Paints, Etc.	2816
		2899
		2851
		3497
		2851
		3952
		2893
551	Essential Oils, Perfumes	2899
		2844
		2899
		2841
553	Perfumery, Cosmetics, Etc.	2844
		2899
		2841
554	Soaps, Cleansing, Etc., Preps	2841
		2843
		2842
582	Products of Condensation, Etc.	2672
		3081
		3089

Table 5-9 continued

583	Polymerization Etc. Products	3082
		3949
584	Cellulose Derivative	No Crossreference
598	Miscellaneous Chemical Products	2842
		3843
		3952
		3299
		3624
		2819
		3295
		2816
		2861
		2611
		2843
		2899
		2865
		3674
		2835
		3291
		3273
		3272
		2869

Table 5-10
SITC #6
Conversion of 3-Digit SITC Numbers Identified as Competitive in Tables 5-6 to 5-8 to 4-Digit SIC Codes

3-Digit SITC #	Description	4-Digit SIC #
611	Leather	3111
642	Paper Etc., Percent of Arts	2676
		2655
		2782
		2761
		2652
		2653
		2673
		2673
		2675
		2679
		2685
		2678
		2621
		2752
		2672
		2955

Table 5-10 continued

651	Textile Yarns	2295
		2281
		2284
		1712
		2824
		3949
		2299
		2231
		3229
655	Knitted Etc, Fabrics	2257
657	Special Textile Fabric Products	2241
		2231
		3069
		2679

Table 5-10 continued

		2295
		2296
663	Mineral Manufacturers NES	3291
		3296
		3295
		3275
		3299
		3269
		3271
		3292
		3842
		3053
		3624
664	Glass	3229
		3211
		3231
		3296
		3564
684	Aluminum	3334
		3399
		3354
		3357
		3353
691	Structures and Parts NES	3441
		3442
		3446
		3444
		3449

Table 5-10 continued

692	Metal Tanks, Boxes, Etc.	3443
		3412
		3499
		3911
696	Cutlery	3421
		3914
621	Materials of Rubber	3052
		3174
		3069
		3011

Table 5-11
SITC #7
Conversion of 3-Digit SITC Numbers Identified as Competitive in Tables 5-6 to 5-8 to 4-Digit SIC Codes

3-Digit SITC #	Description	4-Digit SIC #
711	Steam Boilers Auxiliary Plant	3443
712		3511
716	Rotating Electric Plant	3621
		3511
		3566
718		No Crossreference
721	Agricultural Machinery, Etc., Tractors	3556
		3523
		3521

Table 5-11 continued

		3524
723	Civil Engineering Equipment, ETC.	3531
		9000
		3424
		3532
		3533
727		No Crossreference
728	Other Machinery for Special Industries	3569
		3599
		3559
		3553
		3531
		3585
		3554
737	Metalworking Machinery NES	3548
		3699
		3423
		3547
		3321
		3559
		3542
741	Heating, Cooling Equipment	3569
		3585
		3433
		3556
		3567

Table 5-11 continued

742	Pumps for Liquids, Etc.	3586
		3561
		3714
		3513
		3594
		3593
743	Pumps NES, Centrifuges, Etc.	3563
		3585
		3564
		3714
		3634
744	Mechanical Handling Equipment	3536
		3531
		3534
		3569
		3537
745	Nonecel Machinery Tools NEC	3552
		3554
		3559
		3569
776	Transistor Valves Etc.	3674
		3679
		3671
784	Motor Vehicle Parts Accessories NES	3714
		3523
		3531
		3465

Table 5-11 continued

		3713
785	Cycles, Etc., Motorized or not	3751
		3842
786	Trailers, Non-Motorized Vehicles NES	3715
		3523
		3714
		3792
		3799
		3537
		2451
		3443
793	Ships and Boats, Etc.	9100
		3443
		3069
		3731
		3732
		3728

Table 5-12
SITC #8
Conversion of 3-Digit SITC Numbers Identified as Competitive in Tables 5-6 to 5-8 to 4-Digit SIC Codes

3-Digit SITC #	Description	4-Digit SIC #
871	Optical Instruments	3827
		3699
		3826
872	Medical Instruments NES	3841

Table 5-12 continued

		2599
		3843
		3842
		3949
		3699
874	Measuring Controlling Instruments	3823
		3822
		3694
		3827
		3825
		3812
		3596
		3861
		3569
		3826
		3999
		3545
		3559
892	Printed Matter	2752
		2741
		2771
		9900
		2731
		3944
		2721
		2711
		2672
898	Musical Instruments	3931
		3999
		3652
		9900
		3695

Table 5-13
4-Digit SIC Codes that Cross ReferenceOnly to SITC Codes in Tables 5-6 to 5-8 1981-1992

3-Digit SITC #	Description	4-Digit SIC #
533	Pigment, Plants, Etc.	2851
582	Products of Condensation	2672
621	Materials of Rubber	3052
871	Optical Instruments	2826
892	Printed Matter	2771 2731 2721
898	Musical Instruments	3931 3652 3695

Table 5-14
4-Digit SIC Codes that Cross Reference Only to SITC Codes in Tables 5-6 to 5-8
1981-1987

3-Digit SITC #	Description	4-Digit SIC #
871	Optical Instruments	3826

Table 5-15
4-Digit SIC Codes that Cross Reference Only to SITC Codes in Tables 5-6 to 5-8
1987-1992

3-Digit SITC #	Description	4-Digit SIC #
533	Pigments, Paints, Etc.	2851

Table 5-15 continued

551	Essential Oil Perfumes, Etc.	2844
553	Perfumery, Cosmetics, Etc.	2844
554	Soaps, Cleansing Etc., Preparations	2841
582	Products of Condensation	2672 3081
583	Polymerization Etc. Production	3082
598	Miscellaneous Chemical Products	3299 3624 3674 2835 3273 3272
611	Leather	3111
642	Paper Etc. Precut Arts	2676 2655 2761 2652 2673 2656 2678
651	Textile Yarns	2295 2281

Table 5-15 continued

		2284
655	Knitted Etc. Fabrics	2257
657	Special Textile Fabric Products	2295
		2296
663	Mineral Manufacturers NES	3296
		3299
		3269
		3271
		3053
		3624
664	Glass	3211
		3296
		3564
684	Aluminum	3354
		3353
691	Structures and Parts NES	3441
		3442
		3446
716	Rotating Electric Plant	3621
723	Civil Engineering Equipment	3532
727		3556
728	Other Machinery for Special Industries	3585

Table 5-15 continued

737	Metal Working Machinery NES	3548
		3547
		3321
741	Heating and Cooling Equipment	3585
		3556
		3567
742	Pumps for Liquid Etc.	3586
		3513
743	Pumps for NES Centrifuges Etc.	3563
		3585
		3564
		3634
744	Mechanical Handling Equipment	3536
		3534
745	Non-electric Machine Tools	3565
		3563
		3581
		3546
776	Transistor Valves Etc.	3674
		3671
784	Motor Vehicles Parts Access NES	3465
		3713

Table 5-15 continued

786	Trailer Non-motorized Vehicles NES	3715
		2451
791	Railway Vehicles	3743
		3321
793	Ships and Boats Etc.	3731
		3732
871	Optical Equipment	3826
872	Medial Instruments NES	3841
874	Measuring Controlling Instruments	3822
		3694
		3596
		3569
		3829
		3826
		3545
892	Printed Matter	2741
		2771
		2731
		2721
		2711
		2672
898	Musical Instruments	3931
		3652
		3695

Table 5-16
4-Digit SIC Codes Identified in Table 5-13 and Categorized by Major 2-Digit SIC Group 1981-1992

Major 2-Digit SIC Group & 4-Digit Subgroups	Description
26	Paper and Allied Products
2672	Coated and Laminated Paper NEC
27	Printing and Publishing
2771	Greeting Cards
2731	Books Publishing or Publishing & Printing
2721	Periodicals: Publishing; Printing & Publishing
28	Chemical Allied Products
2826	Optical Instruments
30	Rubber & Misc. Plastic Products
3052	Rubber & Plastic Hose & Belting
36	Electronic & Other Electric Equipment
3652	Phonograph Records & Prerecorded Audio Tapes & Disks
3695	Magnetic & Optical Recording Media
38	Instruments & Related Products
3826	Laboratory & Analytical Instruments
39	Misc. Manufacturing Industries Jewelry, Silverware & Plateware
3931	Musical Instruments

Table 5-17
4-Digit SIC Codes Identified in Table 5-14 and Categorized by Major 2-Digit SIC Group 1981-1987

Major 2-Digit SIC Group & 4-Digit Subgroups	Description
38	Instruments and Related Products
3826	Laboratory & Analytical Instruments

Table 5-18
4-digit SIC Codes Identified in Table 5-15 and Categorized by Major 2-digit SIC Group 1987-1992

Major 2-Digit SIC Group & 4-Digit Subgroups	Description
22	Textile Mill Products
2257	
2281	Yarn Spinning Mills
2284	Thread Mills
2295	Coated Fabrics, Not Rubberized
2296	
24	Lumber & Wood Products
2451	Mobil Homes
26	Paper & Allied Products
2676	Sanitary Paper Products
2672	Coated Laminated Paper not Elsewhere Classified
2655	Fiber Cans, Tubes, Drums, & Similar Products
2652	Setup Paperboard Boxes
2673	Plastics, Foil & Coated Paper Bags
2656	Sanitary Food Containers, Except Folding
2678	Stationary Tablets & Related Products
27	Printing and Publishing
2761	Manifold Business Forms
2741	Misc. Publishing
2731	Books Publishing or Publishing & Printing
2771	Greeting Cards
2721	Periodicals Publishing or Publishing & Printing
2711	Newspapers Publishing or Publishing & Printing
28	Chemicals & Allied Products
2851	Paints. Varnishes, lacquers, Enamels, & Allied Products

Table 5-18 continued

2844	Perfumes, Cosmetics & Other Toilet Preparations
2835	In Vitro & In Vitro Diagnostic Substances
2841	Soap & Other Detergents Except Specialty Cleaners
30	Rubber & Misc. Plastic Products
3053	Gaskets, Packing Devices
3081	Unsupported Plastic Film & Sheets
3082	Unsupported Plastic Profile Shapes
31	Leather & Leather Products
3111	Leather Tanning & Finishing
32	Stone Clay Glass Products
3211	Flat Glass
3271	Concrete
3273	Ready Mixed Concrete
3272	Concrete Products Except Block Brick
3299	Non-metal Mineral Products NEC
3296	Misc.
3269	Pottery Products
33	Primary Pottery Products
3354	Aluminum Extruded Products
3353	Aluminum Sheets, Plate Foil
3321	Gray & Ductile Iron Foundries
34	Fabricated Metal Products
3441	Fabricated Structural Metal
3442	Metal Doors, Sash Frames. Molding & Trim
3446	Oriental Metal Work
3465	Automotive Stampings
35	Industrial Machinery Equipment
3564	Industrial Commercial Fans & Blowers & Air Purification Equipment

Table 5-18 continued

3556	Food Products Machinery
3532	Mining Machinery & Equipment Except Oil & gas Field Machinery & Equipment
3585	Air Conditioning & warm Air Heating Equipment & Commercial & Industrial Refrigerated Equipment
3548	Electric & Gas Welding & Soldering Equipment
3547	Rolling Mill Machinery & Equipment
3567	Industrial Process Furnaces & Ovens
3586	Measuring & Dispensing Pumps
3513	Pumps
3563	Air & Gas Compressors
3534	Elevators & Moving Stairways
3536	Overhead Traveling Cranes & Hoists & Monorail Systems
3565	Packing Machinery
3581	Automatic Vending Machines
3546	Power Driven Hand tools
3569	General Industrial Machinery & Equipment NEC
3596	Scales & Balances Except Laboratory
3545	Cutting Tools, Machine Tool Accessories & Machinists Precision Measuring Devices
36	Electronic & Other Electric Equipment
3634	Electric Housewares & fans
3674	Semi-conductors & Related Devices
3671	Electron Tubes
3624	Carbon & Graphite Products

Table 5-18 continued

3621	Motors & Generators
3652	Phonograph Records & Prerecorded Audio Tapes & Disks
3694	Electrical Equipment for Internal Combustion Engines
3695	Magnetic & Optical Recording Media
37	Transportation Equipment
3713	Trucks & Bus Bodies
3715	Truck Trailers
3743	Railroad Equipment
3731	Shipbuilding & Repairing
3732	Boat Building & Repairing
38	Instruments & Related Products
3826	Laboratory Analytical Instruments
3841	Surgical & Medical Instruments
3822	Automatic Controls for Commercial Environments of Appliances
3829	Measuring & Controlling Devices NEC
39	Misc. Manufacturing Industries Jewelry, Silverware & Plateware
3931	Musical Instruments

Table 5-19
Identifying Competitive Major 2-Digit SIC Groups Determined by the Percentage of Competitive 4-Digit SIC Codes Within Each 2-Digit Code

Major 2-Digit Group	Description	Total of 4-Digit Codes Within 2-Digit Group	of Competitive 4-Digit Codes Identified in tables 28-30	of Competitive 4-Digit Codes to Total 4-Digit Codes	Ranking by %
22	Textile Mill Products	23	5	21.7	9
24	Lumber & Wood Products	17	1	5.9	15
26	Paper & Allied Products	17	7	41.2	2
27	Printing & Publishing	14	6	42.9	1
28	Chemical & Misc. Plastic Products	29	4	13.8	10
30	Rubber & Misc. Plastic Products	15	4	26.6	6
31	Leather & Leather Products	11	1	9.1	14
32	Stone Clay & Glass Products	16	7	26.9	5
33	Primary Metal Industries	26	3	11.5	11
34	Fabricated Metal Products	38	4	10.5	13
35	Industrial Machinery & Other Equipment	51	18	35.3	3
36	Electronic & Other Electric Equipment	36	8	22.2	8
37	Transportation Equipment	18	5	27.8	4
38	Instruments & Related Products	17	4	23.5	7
39	Misc. Jewelry, Silverware & Plateware	18	2	11.1	12

Table 5-20
Three Top Ranked Companies by Sale^tThree Top Ranked Companies by Sales for the 4-Digit SIC Codes in Major 2-Digit Group 27 in 1992

4-Digit SIC Code	Description	Company Name
2711	Newspaper Publishing or Publishing Printing	Times Mirror Co. News America Publishing Inc. Gannett Company Inc.
2721	Periodicals	RR Donneley & Sons Co. McGraw-Hill Inc. Readers Digest Association Inc.
2731	Book Publishing	Thomson Information Publishing Group Simon & Schuster Inc. Harcourt Brace Jovanovich Inc.
2741	Miscellaneous Publishing	Donnelley Directory Bell South Advertising & Publishing NYNEX Information Resources
2761	Mainfold Business Forms	Moore Corporation Ltd. Moore Business Forms Forms & Systems Division Standard Register Co. Uarco Inc.
2771	Greeting Cards	Hallmark Cards Inc. American Greetings Corp. Gibson Greetings Inc.

Ward 1993 Business Directory

Table 5-21
Three Top Ranked Companies by Sales for the 4-Digit SIC Codes in Major 2-Digit Group 27 in 1992

	Description	Company Name
4 Digit SIC Code	Newspaper Publishing and Publishing Printing	Times Mirror Co.
		News America Publishing Inc.
		Gannett Publishing Inc.
2721	Periodicals	RR Donneley & Sons Co.
		McGraw-Hill Inc.
		Reader's Digest Association Inc.
2731	Book Publishing	Thomson Information Publishing Group
		Simon & Schuster Inc.
		Harcourt Brace Jovanovich Inc.
2741	Miscellaneous Publishing	Donnelley Directory
		Bell South Advertising & Publishing
		NYNEX Information Resources
2761	Mainfold Busincess Forms	Moore Corporation Ltd.
		Moore Business Forms Forms & Systems Division
		Standard Register Co. Uarco Inc.
2771	Greeting Cards	Hallmark Cards Inc.
		American Greetings Corp.
		Gibson Greetings Inc.

Ward 1993 Business Directory

Table 5-22
Three Top Ranked Companies by Sales for the 4-Digit SIC Codes in Major 2-Digit Group 35 in 1992

4-Digit SIC Code	Description	Company Name
3513	Pumps	No Cross Reference
3532	Mining Machinery Products	Joy Technologies
		Mine Safety Appliances Co.
		Harnischfeger Corp.
3534	Elevators & Moving Stairways	United Technologies
		Ottis Elevator Co.— United Technologies Corp.
		Dover Corp.
3536	Hoists, Cranes & Monorails	JLG Industries Inc.
		Columbus Mckinnon Corp.
		Mannesmann Demag Corp.
3545	Cutting Tools Machine— Tool Accessories & Machinists Precision Measuring Devices	Smith International Corp.
		GTE Valenite Corp.
		Black & Decker Corp.
3546	Power Driven Hand Tools	Black & Decker Corp.
		U.S. Power Tools Inc.
		Black & Decker Corp.
		SPX Corp.
3547	Rolling Mill Machinery & Equipment	Wean Inc.
		Morgan Construction Co.
		Wean Industries Inc.
		Wean Inc.
3548	Electronic & Gas Welding & Soldering Equipment	Big Three Industries Inc.
		Thermadyne Holding Corp.
		Lincoln Electronic Co.

Table 5-22 continued

3556	Food Products Machinery	Premark International Inc.
		Food Equipment Group
		PMI Food Equipment
		Group Inc.
		Premark International
		Inc.
		Hobart Inc.
3563	Air & Gas Compressors	Thomas Industries Inc.
		Cooper Industries Inc.
		Energy Services Group
		Calmar Spraying
		Systems Inc.
3564	Industrial & Commercial	Snyder General Corp.
	Fans & Blowers & Air	Air & Water
	Purification Equipment	Technologies Corp.
		Snyder General Corp.
		American Air Filter
		Company Inc.
3565	Packaging Machinery	Signode Corp.
		Figgie International Inc.
		Meyer World Packaging
		Manufacturing Co.
		Videojet Systems
		International Inc.
3567	Industrial Process Furnace &	Ogden Projects Inc.
	Ovens	Inductotherm Industries
		Inc.
		Emererson Electric Co.
		El Weigand Division
3569	General Industrial Machinery	Tyco Laboratories Inc.
	NEC	Grinnell Corp.—Tyco
		Laboratories Inc
		Figgie International Inc.

Table 5-22 continued

3581	Automatic Vending Machines	IMI Cornellus (Americas) Inc.
		Dixie-narco Inc.
		Rowe International Inc.
3585	Air Conditioning & Warm Air Heating Equipment & Commercial & Industrial Refrigeration Equipment	Carrier Corp.
		ASI Holding Corp.
		American Standard Inc.
		ASI Holding Corp.
3586	Measuring & Dispensing Pumps	Garco Inc. (Golden Valley Minnesota)
		Tokheim Corp.
		Gilbarco Inc.
3596	Scales & Balances Except Laboratory	Mettier Instrument Inc.
		Chronos Richardson Inc.
		Fairbanks Inc.Fairbank Scales
		Fairbank Inc.

Ward 1993 Business Directory

Table 5-23
Three Top Ranked Companies by Sales for the 4-Digit SIC Codes in Major 2-Digit Group 37 in 1992

4-Digit SIC Code	Description	Company Name
3713	Truck & Bus Bodies	Navistar International Corp.
		Mark Trucks Inc.
		General Motors Corp.
		Truck and Bus Group
3715	Truck Trailers	Terex Corp.
		Fruehauf Trailer Corp.
		Terex Corp.
		International Controls Corp.

Table 5-23 continued

3731	Shipbuilding & Repairing	Newport News Shipbuilding & Dry Dock Co.
		General Dynamics Corp.
		Electric Boat Division Ingalls Shipbuilding Inc.
3732	Boat Building & Repairing	Brunswick Corp.
		Minstar Inc.
		Genmar Industries Inc.
3743	Railroad Equipment—Tool Accessories & Machinists Precision Measuring Devices	Morrison Knudson Corp. (Bosie, Idaho)
		Trinity Industries Inc.
		Duchossois Industries Inc.

Ward 1993 Business Directory

Table 5-24
Three Top Ranked Companies by Sales for the 4-Digit SIC Codes in Major 2-Digit Group 32 in 1992

4-Digit SIC Code	Description	Company Name
3211	Flat Glass	Owens-Illinois Inc.
		Ownes-Illinois Inc.
		Owens-Brockway Glass Containers
		Anchor-Glass Container Group
3269	Pottery Products NEC	Susquehanna Pfaitgraff Co.
		Duncan Enterprises
		Treasure Craft Co.
3271	Concrete Block & Brick	Texas Industries Inc.
		Hydro Conduct Corp.
		Glen-Gery Corp.
3272	Concrete Products NEC	Burke Co.
		Tarmac America Inc.
		Ameron Inc.

Table 5-24 continued

3273	Ready-Mixed Concrete	Florida Rock Industries Inc.
		Beazer West Inc.
		Evered Materials USA Inc.
3296	Mineral Wool	Owens-Corning Fiberglass Corp.
		Owens-Corning Fiberglass Corp. Construction Products Group
		Certain Teed Corp.
3299	Nonmetallic Mineral Products NEC	Hoechst Cermatec North America Inc.
		Howmet Corp.
		Morrison Casting Support Division

Ward 1993 Business Directory

Table 5-25
Three Top Ranked Companies by Sales for the 4-Digit SIC Codes in Major 2-Digit Group 38 in 1992

4-Digit SIC Code	Description	Company Name
3822	Automatic Controls for Commercial Environments & Appliances	General Electric Co. Industrial & Power Systems
		Honeywell Inc.
		Johnson Controls Inc.
3826	Laboratory Analytical Instruments	Perkin-Elmer Corp.
		Beckman Instruments Inc.
		Fisher Scientific

Table 5-25 continued

3825	Measuring & Controlling Devices NEC	IMD Industries Inc.
		Ametek Inc.
		Vishay Intertechnology Inc.
3841	Surgical & Medical Instruments	Baxter International Inc.
		Baxter Health Care Corp.
		Baxter international Inc.
		Siemens Medical Systems Inc.

Ward 1993 Business Directory

Table 5-26
Three Top Ranked Companies by Sales for the 4-Digit SIC Codes in Major 2-Digit Group 30 in 1992

4-Digit SIC Code	Description	Company Name
3052	Rubber & Plastics & Hose Belting	Gates Corp.
		Gates Rubber Co.
		Dayco Products Inc.
3053	Gaskets, Packaging & Sealing Device	BTR Inc.
		Freudenberg NOK
		Fel-Pro inc.
3081	Unsupported Plastics Film & Sheet	Borden Inc.
		Packaging & Industrial Products Division
		Envirodyne Industries Inc.
		ICI Americans Inc.
		ICI Films Group
3082	Unsupported Plastics Profile Shapes	Autostyle Inc.
		Autostyle Plastics Inc.
		Tubed Products Inc.

Ward 1993 Business Directory

NOTES

1. Allen J. Lenz, Narrowing the U.S. Current Deficit, 32.

2. Ibid., 36.

CHAPTER 6

Management Policies That Make Companies Competitive

The demands of the global economy require that a company must simultaneously compete on the product price, quality, and the product line. The manufacturing processes needed to meet those demands require management policies that emphasize participatory management, create an organic organizational structure, and focus on long-term planning horizons. To implement these policies competitive companies made significant changes in their structure, culture, and allocation of resources.

Newport News Shipbuilding and Dry Dock Co. (NNS) is listed in Table 23 as the largest company within SIC code 3731 (ship building and repairing). The company considers—

Its apprenticeship program as a guarantee of world class competitiveness. . . . Most companies that make products have some opportunities for training people at the ground level, but only a few of them really understand what our apprenticeship program really is. . . . It's not training; it's beyond that. The 2,500 apprentices employed by NNS (out of a total work force of 20,000) are the core of the company. They are taught to adapt to the constantly changing nature of technology; they are dedicated to their crafts and the company and evolve from machinist into lifelong learners. . . 70% of the apprentice graduates move Into technical and managerial positions.[1]

Carrier Corporation, listed in Table 22 as the largest company within the SIC code 3585 (air conditioning and warm air heating equipment), developed its newest furnace line by implementing a team model approach. This approach allowed the company to develop a furnace with "the highest efficiency in the industry, in twenty months; about half the normal time."[2]

> The team includes representatives of design, engineering, manufacturing and marketing, working together in an open, dynamic setting to ensure a steady flow of information and feedback. The team members sat together in the same rooms, discussing ideas and working out problems without relying on interoffice mail or the telephone. Team members rode with technicians on service calls listening to how existing units could be improved . As a result 55 new ideas were incorporated into the new furnace lines. . . . These ideas will be aggressively protected with patents.[3]

Carrier during the late 1980s developed several new products, including a thermal ice storage system that is more efficient then conventional systems. It is also developing with GE Plastics a low-cost heating and air-conditioning unit that reduces significantly the emission of refrigerants.

American Greeting Corporation, the second largest company within SIC category 2771 (Table 21), "knows its customers well thanks to the use of the latest technologies and modern management techniques."[4] American Greeting has "moved its manufacturing operations from a functional orientation to just-in-time manufacturing cells. That shift, complete with cross trained personnel, has reduced scrap, cut storage, and increased flexibility."[5]

Hallmark Cards Inc., the largest company within SIC category 2771 (Table 21), reorganized its product development group in the late 1980s in response to reduced profits.

> In the summer of 1991 a new line of cards was developed in an entirely different way. Hallmark grouped people together who had been previously separated by discipline, departments, floors and buildings. The goal was to cut down on the queue time, spur creativity and end the throw-it-over-the-wall-it's-their problem attitude. When you focus a group of people like that you get direct communication and linkage. . . . In the old routine the management committee would periodically review the work of artists and editors. . . . Now the integrated teams review their own work. The

process is not only much faster but we think we are turning out a better product. . . . We are building the organization capability that will enable Hallmark employees to react swiftly and successfully to continuous, unpredictable change.[6]

Ameron Inc., the third largest producer of concrete products (SIC code 3272, Table 241), has made Human Resource Management a critical component of its business strategy. William Craven, Vice President of employee relations at Ameron Inc., states,

It is going to pay and pay well for business to provide training and educational opportunities to employees. . . . Training and re-training is an important function at Ameron. We build pipes which carry millions of gallons of water, oil and gas or whatever. . . . They have to be perfect; we can't make mistakes. . . . It's essential that our employees receive high level technical training.[7]

In reworking the company's benefit package in 1989, Craver notes that "good communication was the key to the success of the new plan. We told the employees every step of the way what we were doing; we were careful to build their trust."[8]

Black and Decker, listed in Table 22 as the largest company within SIC category 3546, has implemented in its Beloit Division Plant a now management technology. "This holistic approach to manufacturing has increased productivity by 70%."[9] The flow management technology integrates well with

an entire array of employee activities and programs that go beyond flow management. There's an entire spectrum including a self-directed employee involvement program, total quality management programs and a process improvement program. But these are not just programs. On the contrary they all blend together to form an overall process. [10]

Under Flow Management Technology—

The supervisor and the manger and the manufacturing engineer all become facilitators. . . . We no longer have a manufacturing engineering department; we have no production control department and we don't have a materials manager. . . . Flow Management has really empowered our people. They do their own scheduling, schedule their own overtime, hire and fire their persons, the whole nine yards."[11]

Black and Decker's household product division has an employee incentive campaign.

It asks volunteer employee teams for ideas. Then it requires these teams to show how to bring the ideas to fruition by performing the preliminary work, estimating costs and learning more about the business... 85% of the eligible employees volunteered for the program... the people were grouped into teams that were made up of members from different departments.... The interaction brought an awareness of the operating challenges of other departments.... The program aims at tapping the abilities of employees, getting them not only to think but to think critically on the job. [12]

SPX, listed in Table 22 as the third largest company within SIC category 3546 (Power Driven Hand Tools), has created a team environment that has empowered employees and coupled it with a continuous improvement management strategy.

The mix of empowerment into a just in time/total quality control environment was implemented in 1986 and has, during the period 1986-1990 increased productivity by 65%, reduced internal scrap rework warranty costs from 4% to .3% of sales and has reduced order to shipping time from two weeks to two to five days.[13]

James Schiltz operating manager notes that, "When there is a hot order a lot of times neither the general manager nor myself hear about it. The sales people go directly to the team people."[14] SPX is introducing this team approach in its European, Australian, and Pacific Rim operations. A member of the Matsuura Company, a Japanese Machine Tool Manufacturer, after a tour of a SPX plant stated that SPX was the most Japanese-like company that he had seen in North America.[15]

Lincoln Electric Co., the third largest electric gas welding and soldering equipment manufacturer (Table 22 SIC 3548), has a guaranteed employment policy. Lincoln has not had a layoff in more than forty years. Every employee with more then two years of service is guaranteed a minimum of thirty hours work per week. The company has its own training program and mostly hires minimally experienced or unskilled employees.[16]

Donald Hasting, CEO of Lincoln, states,

> The company requires that each employee develop self management skills because the company has few layers of management and a high ratio of workers to supervisors. In addition, cross-training employees lets each individual be productive in more than one capacity. . . . The company has enhanced communication between managers and workers through an open-door policy among executives that lets employees bring matters of concern directly to their attention one-on-one and through an employee-elected advisory board which regularly communicates with top management on issues important to employees and the company.[17]

Mr. Hastings further states that "our company is poised for rigorous competition in Europe and other world markets and that domestic demand for our products is at record levels."[18]

Honeywell Inc., listed in Table 25 as the second largest company with SIC category 3822 (automatic controls for commercial environment and appliances), initiated the Honeywell Scarsburough Learning for Life Initiative in 1987, which represents a—

> concerted effort to upgrade the skill and education level of employees. . . . The course they've been taking spearheads the culture changes that must occur to turn the factory into a globally competitive facility. . . . Those changes have to start on the factory floor with the people who directly effect the three aspects of customer satisfaction; on time delivery, product quality and low cost.[19]

The Learning for Life Initiative has facilitated the transition to self directed work teams, JIT management techniques, and total quality management efforts. For the period 1989 through 1992, Honeywell plants using these management techniques showed increases in productivity of 40% to 60% reduction in work in process inventory and 50% reduction in the time from order to delivery to customers.[20]

In 1990 *Industry Week* cited Honeywell Inc. as a company that "creates an environment in which employees are treated as people with a set of real concerns and needs."[21]

Champion International Corporation, Dairy Packaging Division, the second largest producer of Sanitary Food Containers (Table 20 SIC 2656), has implemented a participatory management style in its mill in Quinnesec, Michigan.

> Machine operators are responsible for filling vacancies, handling their own hiring, electing the most worthy employees for promotion and evaluating their own peers. . . . Operators are encouraged to learn multiple tasks. . . we intermingle people in job functions so they can understand the whole process; finance information, order information and sales information is communicated to employees. . . . Champion as a company is committed to participation management.[22]

INNOVATION

The Global economy driven by technology has spawned new learning organizations that innovate faster than ever before.[23]

> Michael Porter concluded that innovation is the critical difference in the ability of companies and nations to achieve competitive advantage. National prosperity is created not inherited and is inextricably linked to how efficiently industry becomes innovative and upgrades. Sony's Akio Morita observed that anyone could come up with an idea but it took a master to profit from its exploitation.[24]

In 1986 the U.S. imported more high tech manufacturing products than it exported. Residents of foreign countries now receive almost half of the patents granted by the U.S. patent office, "and the three corporations registering the most U.S. patents in 1990 were Canon, Toshiba, and Hitachi."[25]

"All evidence available tells us that the conditions for creativity in business owe more to circumstances in which people work and play than any intrinsic difference in genetic coding."[26] The organic structure, participatory management styles, and longer planning horizons that many competitive U.S. companies have developed have allowed them to become more innovative.

The 3M Company listed in Table 20 as the largest company within the SIC category 2672 (coated and laminated paper), "was built on a culture that not only supports but actually encourages innovation."[27]

"Freedom, Sharing of Technologies and Management Sponsorship are all essential ingredients of the lab to market channel of innovation."[28] Innovation at 3M is recognized in a number of ways. The Golden Step program honors cross-functional work teams that introduce successful new products. The Carleton Society, a hall of fame for 3M scientists, honors those who have made long range contributions.

Since the mid 1980s 3M has increased R&D spending from 4.6% of sales to 6.5%, enlarged its research staff from 5,400 to 7,800, and increased the share of money going to basic research.[29] 3M has forty-two divisions with R&D staffs working in over one hundred technologies. In an effort to open communication between these staffs, 3M established a technical forum where specialists in the same scientific discipline, but separate divisions, could meet regularly to share information. 3M also established an annual in-house trade fair where each divisional lab shares its findings.

Yet the lab to market channel is only one route to innovation from which the company derives its growth. Equally important are assessing customer needs and anticipating market trends. All three are increasingly intertwined and essential to innovation. Cross functional teams work closely with customers. For example many of 3M carpet treatments and many of its tape closures for disposable diapers were developed either in joint efforts or in close consultation with carpet fiber makers and diaper makers.[30]

Innovation at Georgia Pacific Corporation, Communication Paper Division (G.P.), the largest manufacturer of stationery products (SIC 2678 Table 201, is focused on utilizing recycled products.

"Products using recycled waste paper are increasingly important for publishers and brochures with a high visibility. They show the public and consumers that companies care about ecological concerns."[31]

New photocopying and printing machines operate at very high speeds and require smoother paper than is obtained by using recycled paper. Georgia Pacific invented a paper machine utilizing "incredibly sophisticated new technologies that can produce paper from recycled products that meet the needs of today's office machines."[32] The machine is fast, cost effective, runs 24 hours a day, and produces more than a thousand tons of paper.

James River, listed in Table 20 as the second largest sanitary paper manufacturer, opened a paper recycling plant in 1991 that is able to "process a wide array of paper grades and to produce high quality pulp."33 The de-inking facility at the plant, i.e., reported to be operating "on the leading edge of recycling technology."[34]

Navistar, the largest manufacturer of trucks and bus bodies (SIC 3713 table 23), introduced in 1990 two heavy duty truck transmissions that represent the first all new design in more than twenty-five years and incorporate several patented features. In 1993 Navistar introduced an electronically controlled fuel injection system. The system was reported to be "the first application of electronic engine control technology for medium duty diesels and a radical departure from conventional diesel design."[35] In 1993 Navistar also invented a new recycling technology that allows it to recycle 300 tons of spent sand per day from the molds and cores it produces. This technology will allow Navistar to exceed current and proposed waste and disposal regulations. It will save 1.4 million feet of landfill per year, and save the company $3 million annually by eliminating the cost of disposing and buying of cores and molds.

Simon and Schuster (S and S) the second largest book publisher (SIC 2731 Table 21), is implementing a systems integration plan. This plan will allow it to have "an in house publishing capability to produce, ship, and store millions of volumes on a near global basis without costly inventory and shipping expense."[36] S and S has bought and installed 3,000 new terminal workstations that range from PC to mid-range computers that are all multifunctional. This technology provides an automated pricing system that helps editors and designers improve cost estimates. . . . Computers make possible a title level profit and loss system far more accurate then any yet available, product time is being halved; book ordering is fully automated and changing the relationship among publishers, booksellers and wholesalers. . . . S & S is now closer to its customers, the Daltons, Waldens and Ingrams.[37]

American Greeting Corp. (Table 21 SIC 2771) has introduced a Create-A-Card system which uses a computerized touch screen that allows a buyer to customize a card from "an almost endless selection of verse and artwork and then watch Create-A-Card finish the full color job."[38] Create-A-Card meets the demands of the global economy, because it allows the customer to tailor a product to his or her own needs.

EFFICIENCY

The manufacturing process and innovations implemented by these companies have allowed them to become more cost effective by enabling them to restructure their operations and reduce their staffs.

Beginning in the mid 1980s Carrier Corporation, as noted earlier, implemented a participatory management style in their efforts to develop and manufacture new products more effectively. In 1992 Carrier announced that it was restructuring its operations, including closing six manufacturing plants, three in North America, and reducing its 28,000 workforce by 1,525 workers.

William Fargo, president of Carrier North American Operation, said the restructuring is a continuation of change made in 1991. He denied that the restructuring was a retrenchment, noting that through the use of new manufacturing process,

> we can make twice as much product now as we could in 1985. We are consolidating product and continuing to install world class manufacturing capability.... The restructuring identifies process improvement, product redesign and purchasing coordination and consolidation as priorities.... The name of the game is speed, responding to the market place and serving customers. A quicker now product cycle allows quicker response. Speeding the ordering cycle provides customer benefits. We can be faster, better and provide higher quality.[39]

Fargo also noted that the restructuring would consolidate administrative functions and—

> allow branch people to concentrate on interfacing with their customers. By eliminating redundant functions we will eliminate the equivalent of 100 positions. Restructuring will reduce the number of suppliers to Carrier North America from 2,500 to 500. ... All will be Q Plan certified to a high quality standard. We want suppliers who are aimed at the same objective as we are. The process of competitiveness is continuous. ... You can't say you're going to stop changing. We have to get out in front of change.[40]

3M underwent considerable restructuring during the mid 1980s, in response to global competitive pressures. It was organized into four sectors which were subsequently reduced to three. The company established a formal strategic planning process which reemphasized the importance of a global perspective and innovation. It established an objective that international sales become 50% of its total sales by 1992 and that 30% of its revenue come from products introduced in the past five years.[41] Five year manufacturing objectives were established to reduce the cost of labor, quality, and production cycle times. In 1990 new objectives were established to reduce the absolute cost of products by a minimum of 10% in five years and to reduce cycle times further. 3M reduced its labor costs and met its goals.

EFFECTIVE RESPONSE TO DEMAND

Many competitive companies restructured their operations when they acquired companies that allowed them to focus on their business core and gain access to foreign markets. Restructuring of other competitive companies resulted from typical U.S. business situations, including divestiture of previous acquisitions obtained as part of a conglomerate strategy that was not successful, the need for cash due to heavy debt incurred from a leverage buyout, or the pressures from financial markets to become more cost efficient and increase returns on investment.

Black and Decker (Table 22 SIC 3546) purchased Emhart Corporation in 1989 and incurred $2.8 billion in debt. To bring its total debt in line with the size of its business Black and Decker sold a number of its business units, including its adhesives operation, shoe materials unit, capacitor unit, and information and electric systems sector. These divestitures, many analysts noted, allowed Black and Decker to focus on its core business. The purchase of Emhart, they believed, transformed Black and Decker into a dynamic global marketing power because a number of business units within Emhart have significant synergy with Black and Decker.[42]

American Standard Inc. (SIC 3585 Table 22), in an attempt to repel a takeover bid by Black and Decker, financed a $3.2 billion leveraged buyout using bank loans and junk bonds. To reduce the debt incurred, the company sold off many of its business units, including its brake division in the U.S. and Europe and its refrigeration division. These sales helped focus the company on its core products: plumbing, air conditioning, and transportation. The need to improve its cash position because of heavy financing costs forced the company to institute a Demand Flow Manufacturing system for all its operations. This system was initially installed to reduce finished goods and raw material inventory levels and the cash needed to maintain them. As part of the Flow Through Manufacturing Process, American Standard instituted a program of participatory management that allowed employees to manage their own part of the production process and actively participate in decision making on the line.... American Standard discovered that this manufacturing process not only reduced inventory levels but more importantly improved efficiencies by 15% to 20%, improved quality, improved responsiveness to customers and helped it gain market share.[43]

Honeywell Inc. (Table 25 SIC 3822) in 1993 reported sales of $6 billion, a drop of $1 billion in revenue from 1988 levels. This reduction was caused by Honeywell divesting itself of acquisitions it made (starting in 1970) in the telecommunications, computer, and semi-conductor industries. The sale of these units allowed Honeywell to focus on its core competency, which is the manufacturing of sensors that detect changes in temperature, pressure, and air flow.

This competency dates from Honeywell's beginning in 1883 when its founder Alfred Butz invented a system for the automatic control of furnace and boiler dampers. It is noted that this restructuring was instigated from the outside by speculator Richard Rainwater who bought a 4% stake in Honeywell in 1988.

Rainwater pressured management into dumping major business units outside the business core under threat of a hostile takeover.... The company used the proceeds from the sale of its business units to retire 30% of its own stock and buyout Rainwater's interest.[44]

Recent acquisitions by Honeywell are linked to its core competence and corporate strategy. Its corporate strategy identifies global business as the primary long-term opportunity for profitable growth. Honeywell has developed an effective global infrastructure including an international management team to meet its objective.

In 1992 Honeywell bought a European company specializing in automating paper making companies. Honeywell was a leader in process controls for pulpmakers but lacked paper quality sensors. This acquisition filled that hole and should increase foreign sales which account for a third of Honeywell's total revenue.[45]

Readers Digest Association Inc. (RDA), listed in Table 21 as the third largest publisher of periodicals within SIC category 2721, installed a new management team in 1985. RDA became a different company under its new bosses. There was a much sharper focus on profits, strategic planning and tighter control. . . . RDA in the late 1980's was characterized by layoffs, lengthened work days and cutbacks in services for employees. . . . The cost cutting measures proved effective as operating margins rose from 3.3% in 1989 to 11.2% in 1990.[46]

In line with its goal of attaining greater efficiencies, RDA in 1992 restructured its business into three operating units, Readers Digest USA and two international units, one covering the Pacific and one covering Europe. Jim Schart, president of RDA, noted that the company will add new products but with limited amounts of new hires. . . . Savings in personnel costs will help fund research for new, projects. . . . RDA management proposes further cost savings in overseas operations where one-half of the company's revenues are generated.[47]

CONCLUSION

The competitive U.S. based companies identified have changed their organizational structure and management practices to meet the demands of the global economy. These changes recognize that the mechanistic structure and autocratic management practices are no longer compatible with today's technology or knowledge workers.

It is noted that these competitive industries are all subject to the pressures of the U.S. business environment and financial markets that reward short-term profits and returns on investment by increasing stock values. These markets punish ill-conceived business strategies such as inappropriate diversification and weak management by reducing stock prices and inviting hostile takeovers.

The nature of the U.S. business environment, which can result in hostile takeovers, changes in management, restructuring, and downsizing has helped many firms become more competitive. This environment has helped these firms to focus on core competencies, install new manufacturing procedures, and implement new management practices. These companies recognize that a balance between short-term operating performance and long-term strategic performance must be achieved to both satisfy the U.S. financial markets and compete in the global economy. The model below,[48] used by Honeywell Inc., is an example of the tools that U.S.-based companies are using to balance short-term and long-term objectives.

Parameters	Scope	Short-term Operational Performance	Long-term Strategic Performance
Objective		Near-term Profits	Competitive Advantage
Assumption		Continuity	Change
Emphasis		Control	Creativity
Document		Budget	Plan
Framework for analysis		Accounting	Accountability through Critical success factors

NOTES

1. Joseph F. McKenna, "Newport News Shipbuilding, Builds More Than Ships," *Industry Week*, November 1, 1993, 39.

2. Wayne Johnson, "Carrier Team Outcomes Furnace Lines with New Products in Only Twenty Months," *Air Conditioning, Heating and Refrigeration News*, July 12, 1993, 6.

3. Ibid., 7.

4. Michael Mturi, "High Tech Makes for High Touch," *Industry Week*, August 19, 1992, 12.

5. Ibid., 12.

6. Robert Buiday, "Re-engineering One Firms Product Development and Anothers Service Delivery," *Planning Review*, March/April 1993, 16.

7. Bill Leavil, "HR Executive Takes a Direct Approach," *HR Magazine*, February 1990, 51.

8. Ibid., 54.

9. Robin P. Bergstrom, "Maybe You Simply Need to Change Lanes" *Production*, February 1992, 48.

10. Ibld., 48

11. Ibid., 48.

12. Steven Paloncy, "Team Approach Cuts Costs," *HR Magazine*, November 1990, 61.

13. Joseph McKenna, "SPQ", *Industry Week*, October 21, 1991, 49.

14. Ibid., 50

15. Ibid., 50.

16. Toni Perry. "Staying with the Basics." *HR Magazine*. November 1990, 73.

17. "A Blueprint to ISO 9000," *Machine Dealing*, October 22, 1993, 226

18. Ibid., 226.

19. Norman Ropper, "Reinventing the Factory with Lifelong Learning," *Training*, May 1993, 55.

20. Ibid., 55.

21. Michael Verespy, "World Class Organizations," *Industry Week*, January 16, 1990, 22.

22. *Pulp and Paper*, May 1992, 79.

23. Joel D. Goldhar and David Lei, "The Shape of Twenty First Century Global Manufacturing," *The Journal of Business Strategy*, March/April 1991, 58

24. "Incorporating a Creative Culture," *International Management*, May 1990, 82.

25. "Corporate R&D", *FW*, October 1, 1991, 32.

26. "Incorporating A Creative Culture," *International Management*, May 1990, 82.

27. Ronald Mitch, "Three Roads to Innovation", *The Journal of Businens Strategy*, September/October 1990, 18.

28. "Corporate R&D", *FW*, October 1, 1991, 32.

29. "Corporate R&D", *FW*, October 1, 1991, 32.

30. Ronald Mitch, "Three Roads to Innovation," *The Journal of Business Strategy*, September/October 1990, 20.

31. Christopher Sheehan, "Two Avenues of Growth for the Paper Industry," *The Office*, November 1991, 56.

32. Ibid., 56.

33. "Turning a New Leaf In Recycling of Office Waste Paper," *The Office*, November 1991, 56.

34. Ibid., 21.

35. "Delivery Under Pressure," *Automotive Industries*, December 1993,

36. Thomns Weyr, "The Wiring of Simon and Schuster," *Publishers Weekly*, June 1, 1992, 33.

37. Ibid., 33.

38. Joseph Mckenna, "From JIT With Love." *Industry Week*, August 17. 1992, 45.

39. Wayne Johnson, "Carrier Says Cutback will Help It Compete." *Air Conditioning, Heating and Refrigeration News*, January 27, 1992, 3.

40. Ibid., 4.

41. "Product Development Minnesota Mining and Manufacturing," *FW*, September 28, 1993.

42. *Lawn and Garden Marketing*, September 1990, 44.

43. Michael Barrier, "When "Just In Time" Just Isn't Enough," *Nations Business*, November 1992, 30.

44. Norrn Alster, "In Fighting Trim," *Forbes*, June 10, 1991, 51.

45. Marcla Berss, "Under Control," *Forbes*, January 31, 1994, 51.

46. Warren Bergor, "The McLaughiln Legacy Condensing Digest," *Fozio*, Feburary 1991, 44.

47 Jim Milliot, "Readers Digest Focusing on Cost Containment In 1994," *Publisher Weekly*, November 15, 1993, 22.

48. F. Paul Carlson. "The Long and Short of Strategic Planning." The Journal of Business Strategy, May/June 1990, 18. 16.

CHAPTER 7

Public and Private Sector Policy Implications

While many U.S.-based industries were losing global market share during the 1970s and 1980s, many government official, business leaders, and economists urged the federal government to take a more active and direct role in helping U.S. industries against foreign-based competitors. The findings of this paper show that while only two 3-digit SITC categories reported export market share growth in excess of import market share growth for the period 1981-1987, forty-four 3-digit SITC categories reported export market share growth in excess of import market share growth for the period 1987-1992. This dissertation has therefore determined that U.S. industries made significant gains against foreign competitors during the period 1987-1992 without the implementation of an industrial policy.

A CASE FOR AN INDUSTRIAL POLICY

The advocates of a U.S. industrial policy looked for role models to the Japanese and European governments, which had supportive relationships with their domestic-based industries. The Japanese Ministry of International Trade and Industry (MITI) "functions as a promoter and protector of industries more than as a regulator and has consistently pursued the policy of aiding and supporting business and industry."[1]

Underlying the effectiveness of a national industrial policy is the concept of strategic trade theory. This theory proposes that actual trade does not necessarily operate according to natural comparative advantage especially in advanced goods that can be produced anywhere; Semi-conductors are not like bananas. . . . Moreover, advantage can be captured and even created by governments.[2]

International competition is now influenced by national strategies as well as strategies of firms. And the history of the last thirty years makes it clear that a developmental strategy based on mobilizing the resources of a nation to create comparative advantage in growth industries and industries in which technological change is rapid, yields higher growth over the medium term than simply accepting advantages as given.[3]

Governments that target critical industries can create comparative advantage. France has practiced targeting almost as long as Japan, beginning with similar concepts based on wartime rationing and using similar control mechanisms including credit control and administrative guidance. And like Japanese firms, large French firms basically accepted that government should consult with industry and give guidance from time-to-time.[4]

In the U.S., with its Jeffersonian and individualistic roots, targeting of industries implies national planning.

> There is widespread resistance to what could be and has been called national planning, variously due to doubts as to its efficacy, to fear of adverse effects on our market system, to political beliefs about government intervention in our economic system and to the current emphasis on short-term returns in both the political and economic arenas.[5]

The U.S. government has historically become involved in the affairs of business only when political constituencies urge government to protect them from the power of business. Industry specific regulations dictated by independent regulatory commissions, antitrust laws, government directed activities like OSHA, and various civil rights commissions promote an adversarial relationship between government and business. Antitrust laws make it difficult for a firm to gain control of its markets. Businesses subject to discrimination, safety laws, and rate of return criteria imposed by regulatory commissions resent government intrusion into fundamental managerial decisions.

In response to the difficulties experienced by many U.S. industries in the 1970s, the government pursued sometimes contradictory policies. It attempted to assist businesses but also pacify political constituencies that wanted business to respond to their particular needs. During the period 1975-1983, domestic market share of U.S.-based auto makers fell from 86% to 71%. The global market share fell from 27% in 1975 to 17% in 1982. In 1982, 270,000 members of the United Auto Workers were laid off indefinitely as employment by U.S. auto makers dropped from 1.03 million in 1978 to 685,000 in 1982.[6] The government's response to this problem was inconsistent. The federal government negotiated voluntary import restrictions to alleviate the pressure from foreign competitors and at the same time "it had decided to make matters of public policy—safety, the environment, social justice, energy—high priorities without consideration of the cost or competitive implications."[7]

The U.S. government's relationship to its steel industry, compared to the role played by foreign governments toward their steel industries, is given as a major reason by many analysts for the decline of the U.S. steel industry. During the 1950s, steel imports averaged about 1.7% of domestic consumption, and by the 1970s steel imports averaged between 18%-22% of domestic consumption.[8] The U.S. government did negotiate voluntary import restraints and developed trigger pricing to discourage dumping by foreign steel companies; these strategies were effective from time-to-time. At the same time the government also pressed for early settlement of strikes and jawboned down steel price increases that had an adverse effect on costs and investments. It also enforced anti-trust policies that prevented necessary restructuring of the industry.[9] No other competitive country has adopted a stance that is basically adversarial toward its steel industry. Abroad, government involvement is pervasive, in the form of quotas, tariffs, preferential procurements, subsidies of all forms, and a variety of other measures to control trade.[10]

The U.S. attempt to cope with trade imbalance in the textile industry has been ineffective also. U.S. imports of textiles and apparel rose from 306 million pounds in 1961 to 1.2 billion pounds in 1972 and to 2.2 billion pounds in 1983. As imports rose, the balance of trade in textiles and apparel deteriorated from a trade deficit of $191 million in 1961 to $2.4 billion in 1972 and to $9.6 billion in 1983.[11] The U.S. government's response to rising imports and increased deficits was the negotiation of a Multifiber Arrangement (MFA) in 1974. The MFA was a multilateral agreement negotiated under GATT and endorsed by fifty countries. It authorized unilateral restrictions against imports that disrupt or threatened to disrupt the U.S. market.

> The MFA is not viewed by the U.S. government as an instrument to reduce or maintain existing levels of textile and apparel imports . . . but to promote the orderly growth of the textile trade among countries on a sound nondisruptive basis.[12]

The MFA did not prevent the continued deterioration of the apparel and textile trade deficit during the 1970s and early 1980s nor did the U.S. take an active role in restoring the competitiveness of the industry during this period.

> The government does not view its role as being responsible for strengthening the competitiveness of individual U.S. industries; it does not act as a catalyst for solving industry wide solutions. No government official has a mandate to help an industry prepare an adjustment plan, nor would a government rote of this kind be generally welcomed in the private sector. Thus, there is no detailed consultation between labor and government as to how relief would be utilized.[13]

In Europe, political leaders built on an established tradition of a strong centralized government in developing postwar industrial policies. In Japan, a relationship between bureaucrats, government, and business that had evolved since the Meiji Dynasty facilitated the development of an effective business-government partnership.

The Ministry of International Trade and Industry (MITI) is Japan's coordinating ministry for industrial policy. "The ministry has the powerful backing not only of industry but also of trade associations and the four big business organizations that are in effect its constituency."[14]

> The basis of MITI's power over industry lies in its ability to withhold licenses and legal permission whenever companies balk at its wishes. Information guidelines concerning one area of business are often heeded because of an implied threat to withhold cooperation in another area that the firm may want to venture into.[15]

With the cooperation of business leaders and politicians, MITI has been able to direct resources toward the high tech end of the industrial sector for the past forty years. Industrial policy in Germany and Japan has the following components:

A strategy agreed upon by industry, banks and governments.

Facilitation of growth of selected industry segments.
Facilitation of the phasing out of selected industrial segments.[16]

THE U.S. VERSION OF AN INDUSTRIAL POLICY

Special Government Subsidies and Credits

Many politicians, business leaders, and economists criticized the U.S. government for not taking a more active role in assisting U.S. industries during the 1970s. The structure, history, and ideology is not present for an activist government role in industrial relations. Instead, U.S. involvement has been focused on a wide assortment of government subsidies, special tax provisions, and subsidized loans and guarantees. Special tax credits and tax depreciation allowances going to specific industries increased from $7.9 billion in 1950 (1% of GNP) to $62.4 billion in 1980 (3% of GNP).[17] " In 1950, the cost to the government of subsidized loans and loan guarantees to specific industries was only $300 million. By 1980, the annual cost had grown to $3.6 billion."[18] The financial bailouts of Chrysler and Lockheed were successful, but they were approved only after a hard struggle in Congress. The assistance given to these companies was considered, even by congressmen who voted for it, as an intrusion in the free market, an exception that should not be the basis of a more activist government.

> All government assistance to business and to individual citizens is seen as somehow illegitimate, the government is forced to respond to each industry's plea for assistance as if it were an exceptional case and to respond to all such requests with special emergency interventions.[19]

In the 1980s, the Reagan and Bush Administrations continued to provide a wide assortment of government subsidies and tax credits to business, but they were categorically opposed to the type of industrial policy practiced in Europe and Japan. Their policy was to liberate the free market from the remnants of government interference. The prevailing free market philosophy would not permit the Department of Commerce to call in the major auto makers, steel makers, or consumer appliance/manufacturers and their bankers and suppliers and coordinate a policy for maintenance of domestic market share or penetration of foreign markets.

National Defense

A U.S. industrial policy, if there is to be one, must be based on the philosophical and ideological roots of the U.S. and the historical relationship between business and government. The basis of an industrial policy for the U.S. could lie in the post World War II national defense policy. The Only experience the U.S. has with national industrial strategy is with national defense.

> The Eisenhower Administration's highway building program—called the National Defense Highway Act of 1956—justified on national security grounds—provided an infrastructure that guided and accelerated post war industrial development particularly for the automobile and housing industries. Similarly, education programs and subsidies embodied in the GI Bill and later in the National Defense Education Act spurred great advances in America's store of human capital which in turn contributed to our economic development well into the 1960s.[20]

Traditionally the construction of highways has been a concern primarily of state and local governments. After decades of discussion however the federal government in 1966 became more directly involved in financing highway construction with a commitment to shoulder 90% of the cost of 41,000 miles of interstate and defense highways. . . . The national network of 4-lane highways would be completed at a cost of approximately $100 billion . . . they constituted a valuable extension of the nation's transportation system. . . . But the expenditures could not have been made had they not been justified in terms of their contribution to the nation's cold war defense.[21]

Investments in the infrastructure absorbed over 6% of the nation's nonmilitary federal budget during the 1950s and 1960s.

> Public spending on the nation's transportation system declined in the 1970s and declined even more sharply in the 1980s to the point where the nation was spending only 1.2% of its nonmilitary budget (about 3% of GNP) on building and maintaining the infrastructure. . . . By the end of the 1980s Washington was annually investing about the same amount of money in infrastructure (in constant dollars) as it invested 30 years before although the GNP had grown 144% in the interim. . . . In 1989 the Department of Transportation estimated that

simply to repair the nation's 240,000 bridges would require an expenditure of $50 billion, to repair the nation's highways, $315 billion.[22]

"Our transportation infrastructure has decreased to the point where it can be a significant inhibitor to economic progress."[23] Advocates of an industrial policy urge the federal government to improve the infrastructure for economic purposes as it had for defense reasons during the Eisenhower administration.

The U.S. science policy instituted after World War II was aimed at winning the Cold War. . . . It emphasized improving education and the U.S. scientific infrastructure and expanding the frontiers of knowledge. It focused on building up the American supply of scientific talent and equipment. That post war policy did strengthen the U.S. R&D base, establish national laboratories and research facilities on an unparalleled scale and create an unequaled pool of technical talent.[24]

Prior to 1940 most of the financial support for scientific and engineering disciplines had come from state governments through their educational institutions or from private foundations, individuals and business. These sources had sufficed to build an elaborate network of professional disciplines, associations, publication and research organizations in this country. . . . During the years 1900-1940, American Science and Engineering had as a result achieved high international stature for the first time in the nation's history.[25]

During the war the Federal government pumped large sums of money into and recruited talented personnel for military projects many of which achieved impressive technical and scientific results. Large scale efforts such as the one that produced the atomic bomb and those that developed advanced radio systems were extremely successful, as were a large number of smaller ventures funded by the government. This successful experience led in the late 1940s to a substantial federal investment in science and engineering largely channeled through existing academic and professional institutions. Once again the results were outstanding. The U.S. became the international leader in many of the most important disciplines including physics and biology. . . . Business benefited directly and indirectly from the post war expansion of the science-technology network. . . . Corporate R&D departments recruited trained personnel from schools and laboratories supported with state and federal funds. . . . Ideas generated in the public sector could be used to commercial advantage. . . . For instance much of the early research on microwave transmissions was sponsored by the government; in the postwar years microwave devices have revolutionized communication.[26]

In reaction to the Soviet Union's launch of Sputnik, the Pentagon created the Advanced Research Projects Agency (ARPA) in 1958. "ARPA's task was ending interservice rivalry in high tech especially in the U.S. space effort."[27] When Congress created NASA to guide the space program, ARPA became the Pentagon's technology mission agency and was renamed the Defense Advanced Research Project Agency (DARPA). "In the 1960s and 1970s DARPA was the Defense Department's anti-surprise Agency, intended to ensure that something like Sputnik didn't surprise the U.S. again."[28] Despite having no labs of its own, DARPA's dispersal of military contracts has made it a critical player in civilian sciences and engineering. "DARPA's main mode of operation is in the two to ten year kind of project that starts out when someone has an idea that has potential for tremendous impact. The project ends with a concept demonstration or a prototype or a technology demonstration."[29]

These are the projects that have the most difficulty attracting private investment but have the potential to produce new industries. Funding by DARPA of projects through private companies has facilitated the raising of private capital because DARPA lends credibility to these research projects. Barrons observed that DARPA is "by far the biggest venture capital fund in the world."[30] Computer technologies, including artificial intelligence, interactive computers, graphics, time sharing, and computer security systems, were developed initially through DARPA funding. The whole field of material science came out of DARPA's initial investment in a dozen interdisciplinary research labs. By the late 1980s DARPA was funding joint efforts, in partnership with industry, in areas such as high definition displays, high speed chips, specialized lasers, computer networks, and infrared sensors.

In 1986 Casper Weinberger, the Secretary of Defense, was shocked to learn that half the chips in the F-16 fighter's fire control radar came from Japan. . . . American companies simply could not make the chips to the specifications required. American companies had not kept up. Hitachi, Toshiba, and Mitsubishi Electronic had been improving their technology while U.S. semi-conductor firms had lost $2 billion in earnings and 27,000 jobs between 1980-1986.[31]

In response to a perceived national security threat, the government passed legislation (in mid-1987) that founded the Semiconductor Manufacturing Technology Initiative (SEMATECH), a Texas based consortium of fourteen major semiconductor manufacturers.

"The member companies account for more than 75% of the semiconductor manufacturing capacity in the U.S. The $200 million per year cost of operating SEMATECH is shared equally by the member companies and the Department of Defense, through DARPA (renamed ARPA in 1993)."[32]

SEMATECH is focused on the process of manufacturing. It has devoted much of its efforts to beefing up the 130 or so American companies that supply most of the tools for processes such as photolithography, chemical etching and molecular epitany. SEMATECH is also developing new manufacturing techniques at a state of the art fabrication line. . . . Last fall it turned out its first batch of chips with a resolution of a 0.5 microns, an achievement SEMATECH officials say brings them even with their Japanese competitors.[33]

SEMATECH's explicit goal is to develop and test advanced fabrication techniques for a new generation of semi conductor chips and to promote their diffusion throughout the U.S. electronic industry. SEMATECH's ultimate aim is to enable U.S. producers of semiconductor devices to surpass their foreign rivals in manufacturing efficiency and quality for future generations of widely used integrated circuits.[34]

SEMATECH's establishment has coincided with a turnaround in the semiconductor industry. After nearly a decade of falling world market share and U.S. firms being overtaken by Japanese firms, the relative U.S. decline was reversed in 1989. "In 1992 the U.S. won a larger share of the world market than Japan for the first time since

1985, and U.S. firms took the leading positions in both the semiconductor and equipment markets."[35] Though it is widely accepted that SEMATECH has had a influence in the turnaround, it is more difficult to determine its contributions.

> No SEMATECH members contacted by Science Magazine were willing to claim they'd increased their market share as a result of SEMATECH advances. But spokespersons for IBM, Digital Equipment and Motorola practically radiate with enthusiasm over SEMATECH's progress. There is a tremendous sense that SEMATECH is doing the right thing says Paul Bergevin, an IBM spokesmen.[36]

When the GAO asked member companies to list SEMATECH's most important initiatives, partnering for the total quality project and the equipment improvement program came up repeatedly. . . . Several member companies stated that one of SEMATECH's most important contribution was as Q forum for communication, enabling members to discuss manufacturing problems and solutions.[37]

Some analysts indicate that a shift in market share is due to the Japanese economic recession arid entry into the market of other Asia/Pacific producers. These producers focus on memory chips, which is Japan's strongest area, while the U.S. dominates the microprocessor market.[38]

National Cooperative Research Act

The development of business-government consortia in the U.S. stems from the National Cooperative Research Act (NCRA) which was enacted in 1984. The Act was primarily a response to heavy lobbying by computer firms that claimed that the Japanese government's $1.3 billion fifth generation computer project would devastate the U.S. computer industry.

> The NCRA encourages cooperative R&D efforts at the precompetitive stage of production by limiting the anti-trust exposure of consortia that file with the Department of Justice. Precompetitive research encompasses experimentation and study of phenomenon and observable facts, development or testing of engineering techniques,

development of prototypes and models and the exchange of research information.[39]

Japan and Western European countries encourage collaboration of competitors and government to achieve technological advances. The Japanese provide government-backed loans and research subsidies as well as encourage the pooling of technical and scientific talent to promote R&D. The European community's liberal exemptions from anti-trust regulation also encourage R&D consortia. The major barrier preventing the emergence of R&D consortia in the U.S. has been anti-trust legislation.

Business consortia were prevalent in the U.S. in the nineteenth century, when U.S. companies within a given industry would join together to pursue their mutual interest. These consortia were outlawed by the Sherman Anti-Trust Act of 1896. Upon the passage of the NCRA, firms within industries began forming R&D consortia. As of August 1989, 137 R&D consortia were registered. Consortia have been formed in the computer and telecommunication industries, in agriculture, automotive, steel, machine tools, biotechnology, chemical, and glass industries.[40]

Industry consortia are relatively new organizations and have experienced difficulties evaluating output and reconciling equity concerning the pooling of resources required to fund precompetitive research. Short product life cycles and rapid advances in technologies require high capital and R&D necessities, which are incentives for cooperation in a noncompetitive infrastructure. Consortia also present a funding mechanism for government agencies such as DARPA.

In response to increased imports the National Center for Manufacturing Science (NCMS) was formed in 1986 as a R&D consortium for the machine tools industry. "The import share of the U.S. domestic market, for machine tools increased from 23% in 1980 to an all time high of nearly 50% in 1986; in 1990 it stood at 49%."[41] The mission of the NCMS was to develop advanced processing technologies for a wide range of materials and promote their widespread use within U.S. industries. Citing defense preparedness as a concern, the Reagan Administration provided $5 million per year in matching grants to NCMS for fiscal years 1988 -1990.[42] Since the early 1980s, the federal government has been involved in several joint R&D efforts with the steel industry, including exploring methods for "directly reducing iron ores into steel, development of superplastic steel and the near-net-shape casting of low carbon steel sheet."[43]

A predecessor of the R&D consortium is the Industry/University Cooperative Research Center (IUCRC). IUCRC's are initiated by the university and initially funded by the federal government. The federal funds are used to attract enough industry members to make the IUCRC self-sustaining. The universities, however, have substantial input into how the centers operate. The Semiconductor Research Cooperative (SRC) was established in 1982. It sought to enhance semiconductor research in U.S. universities. SEMATECH has close links to SRC and provides 1/3 of its funding. Links between industry and universities date back to the land grant colleges when agricultural research projects helped improve agricultural output. During World War II Federal government funded projects at MIT, and the University of Chicago provided the basic research for the atomic bomb. The funding of projects during this period at Stanford helped begin the communication revolution.

PROPOSALS ADVANCED BY ADVOCATES OF INDUSTRIAL POLICY IN THE U.S.

Education Reform

While R&D consortia and university/industry cooperative research centers may facilitate technological advances that help U.S. industries compete, an improved education system will provide U.S.-based companies with a competitive work force.

> Motorola estimates that it has interviewed nearly 40,000 applicants to fill 4,000 factory jobs at its new cellular manufacturing plant in Libertyville, Illinois just north of Chicago. It still has 1,000 vacancies for $10-$15 per hour jobs. Now the company must find another 3,000 workers to operate a one million square foot cellular plant it is building in Harvard, Illinois to take direct aim at the newly opened Japanese market. This is the plant where we will build the cellular phones that will penetrate the Japanese market. . . . The scarcity of qualified workers is not confined to entry level jobs, company officials say the shortage of electronic technicians had forced it to experiment with a program that compresses the studies of a two year community college into a 14 week training course.[44]

The emergence of a technical class in manufacturing has created a paradox in the work place.

At the same time that many employees are having a hard time finding the workers with skills they need, 14 million Americans are either unemployed or involuntarily working part time. . . . Motorola says it is rejecting 9 out of 10 job applicants as unqualified for the company's factories and has spent $30 million in the last 5 years on literacy training alone."[45]

Education is generally considered the responsibility of government. "Of the $2.3 billion that corporations contributed to education in 1989 only $400 million went to support the public schools; the rest went to colleges and universities." [46]

The American education system in the post World War II era fit nicely into the prevailing structure of high volume production.

American schools mirrored the national economy with standard assembly line curriculum divided neatly into subjects taught in predictable units of time arranged sequentially by grade and controlled by standardized tests intended to weed out defective units and return them for reworking. . . . By the 1990s the average American child was ill-equipped to compete in the high value global economy but within that average was a wide variation. American children as a whole are behind their counterparts in Canada, Japan, Sweden and Britain in mathematical proficiency, science and geography.[47]

The failure of the American school to deliver universal literacy is America's real "Rust Belt". It is a far greater weakness than high cost and poor quality in consumer products. In the knowledge society, the knowledge base is the foundation of the economy.[48]

Only 15%-20% of American children are being prepared for a lifetime of work in the global economy. A majority of these children attend high quality suburban public schools; they are tracked through advanced courses and have access to state of the art laboratories, interactive computers, and video systems. Their classes are relatively small and their peers intellectually stimulating. At home they have educational books, toys, videotapes, microscopes, and computers.[49]

Unlike European and Japanese schools which are held accountable for their performance through competitive parallel school systems or performance grading systems, the American school system has little competition. However, American public education does have performance standards and maintains competition among schools in various regions throughout the country; U.S. schooling has done an acceptable job of delivering universal literacy.[50]

The new technician class requires training beyond high school to qualify for jobs at Motorola and other high tech factories. Apprenticeship programs similar to those in Germany, that tie into high school and post high school technical curricula, could improve the work readiness of U.S. school children. "Japan's greatest education success has been to ensure that even its slowest learners achieve a relatively high level of proficiency."[51]

An active role by the Federal government in post secondary education has an historical precedent, dating from land grant colleges and funding of research projects. Elementary and secondary education has been primarily entrusted to local and state governments. These agencies have failed to improve apprenticeship programs or update curricula to meet today's needs. Some education leaders argue that tying teacher's incomes to rising performance standards, currently being done in Rochester, New York, and instituting a voucher system in which the state pays a child's tuition to any accredited school, are steps that will force change. Developing nationwide standards and providing federal tax credits or subsidies to companies that participate in apprenticeship programs are ideas that have also been suggested.

Tax and Regulatory Reform

Advocates of an industrial policy argue that the federal government should take a more active role in elementary and secondary education by revising curriculum and apprenticeship programs and providing equipment to schools similar to equipment found in quality suburban schools. They note that during the 1980s federal support for elementary and secondary education dropped by one-third. By the late 1980s, America's per pupil expenditure (converted to dollars using 1988 exchange rates) was below per pupil expenditures in eight other nations, including Japan, West Germany, and Canada.

Advocates of increased federal involvement in industrial matters argue that the tax and regulatory treatment of America's financial markets needs to be reformed so that they no longer emphasize short-term return at the expense of long-term investment in technologies, production processes, and people.

> The U.S. financial environment is not hospitable to long term investment in technologies and equipment. High capital costs and pressures from financial markets favor taking short-term profits rather than investing for the longer run. Moreover the terms on which capital equipment is made available are more favorable to long-term investment in both Japan and Germany.[52]

The U.S. tax system has fewer incentives for productivity enhancing investments in manufacturing than those of its competitors, especially Japan. Investment and R&D tax credits and capital gains differentials are tax policies that many business leaders and economists believe would encourage investment in manufacturing and increase productivity. The National Coalition for Advanced Manufacturing, a group of 18 leading trade groups, urged that a—

> 10% modernization tax credit be given for new or refurbished plants and equipment; an additional 5% credit to firms with fewer than 500 employees that intend to modernize, and a 5% credit be given to qualified manufacturing companies that have realized a productivity gain of 5% or more during the previous tax year period.[53]

To lower capital costs, many analysts urge that all individual savings be free from taxes and a stock dividend deduction be allowed which favors equity financing over debt financing.

To encourage long-term planning, the SEC has been urged to eliminate short-term earnings reports of publicly owned companies. Advocates of this policy recommend "shifting first to only semi-annual reports with annual reporting only phased in over a two- to three-year period."[54] Proponents argue that by extending the period between earnings reports, managers would have a greater opportunity to focus on long-term strategic goals.

By relaxing anti-trust laws, the government has encouraged the development of R&D consortia and has created a mechanism that allows it to fund research projects in selected critical industries.

By further relaxing anti-trust laws to allow joint product ventures many small and medium size U.S. firms especially in high technology industries can achieve a scale of production and flexibility and raise the capital needed to stay competitive while pooling the substantial risks involved in bringing new technologies into the market.[55]

At the same time, a government agency like DARPA could help fund projects of these joint product ventures as it does the R&D consortia.

Advocates of an industrial policy urge the federal government to increase its funding of education and the infrastructure. They also urge the development of a national technology policy and tax and regulatory reform as a means of extending the influence of the federal government and improving industrial competitiveness.

The Clinton Administration appears to be proceeding toward a national industrial policy. It is proposing apprenticeship programs and national education standards and is increasing the funding for the infrastructure, including the development of an information highway. The Administration has changed the name of DARPA back to ARPA to recognize that half of its funding supports technology that is applicable to the commercial sector.

The Administration has given the Department of Commerce through the Advanced Technology Program (ATP) the authority to fund precompetition R&D projects that are targeted for commercial use. The National Institute of Standards and Technology, a bureau of the Department of Commerce, has been assigned the task of administering the ATP and working with industry to develop innovating technologies. The ATP budget is expected to grow from $68 million in 1992 to $750 million in 1997 and will fund projects using procedures that are similar to those used by DARPA.[56]

THE CASE AGAINST AN INDUSTRIAL POLICY

Opponents of industrial policy warn that an increase in funding for education and infrastructure projects will increase the budget deficit and/or raise taxes and ultimately hurt the competitiveness of U.S. industries. These analysts note that—

a case might be made for some continued government research funding in universities and for specific projects in corporate labs. But that money should not be funneled through the Commerce Department. . . . Under Commerce, grants will soon become political pork. . . . Though there is evidence of successful government sponsored research, there is next to none that government investment is more farsighted or more efficient than that done by the private sector.[57]

It is further noted by opponents of industrial policy that government regulations in areas such as health, safety, and the environment have increased the cost of doing business and have hurt U.S. competitiveness.[58] Industrial policy critics argue that SEMATECH is helping the wrong people and is irrelevant to the gains made by start-ups in the semi-conductor industry, and its tangible accomplishments are meager. SEMATECH, they say, demonstrates that government intervention works no better in hi-tech industries than in the textiles, agriculture, and automobile industries.[59]

Critics of industrial policy acknowledge that the education system must be improved and that the infrastructure must be upgraded in order for the U.S. to compete in the global economy. They also acknowledge that through strategic trade policies foreign governments have created competitive advantage for their critical industries. Underlying arguments against industrial policy, and also a concern of those supporting an industrial policy, is whether "the U.S. with its tradition of fragmented government and hostile business-government relations suffers from a comparative disadvantage in conducting industrial policy competently."[60]

Advocates of industrial policy support the creation of a lead agency to plan and carry out a coherent strategy: High reward industries are selected for particular attention, and elements of technology, trade, and financial policies are combined as needed.[61] Critics argue that there already are cabinet level posts for Labor, Trade, Commerce, Education, and the Treasury and that another layer of bureaucracy will not create competency. Others note that:

Whatever bureaucratic arrangement is chosen matters less than the substance of the strategic policies and the commitment of both the Administration and Congress. No arrangement will solve all coordination problems; there are always competing government objectives. And no arrangement will create a U.S. equivalent of Japan's powerful Ministry of International Trade (MITI). What it could do is make possible a modest start in pulling together policy strands that would promote critical industries and our national economic welfare.[62]

The roots of American culture and ideology will prevent the implementation of an industrial policy unless U.S.-based firms and critical industries become non-competitive to the point of threatening our national security. Until that time U.S. government will not provide the same level of assistance foreign governments provide to their industries and firms. Many U.S.-based firms, beginning in the late 1980s developed and implemented, on their own, strategies and management policies and practices that have made them competitive in the global economy.

These companies have become competitive by adapting participatory management styles and organic organization structures with innovation and long-term planning horizons becoming part of their corporate culture. These companies have restructured their operations, cut costs, and become more efficient.

The changes that competitive companies made in the late 1980s and early 1990s served as a model for other U.S.-based companies and led to improved U.S. global competitiveness a healthy domestic economy.

NOTES

1. Karel Van Wolferen, *The Enigma of Japanese Power*, 125.

2. Robert Kuttner, "Facing up to Industrial Policy," *New York Times Magazine*, April 19, 1992, 26.

3. Bruce R. Scott and George C. Lodge, *U.S. Competitiveness in the World Economy*, 138-139.

4. Ibid., 132.

5. "National Industrial Policy," *Congressional Digest*, December 1992, 298.

6. Bruce R. Scott and George C. Lodge, *U.S. Competitiveness in the World Economy*, 191.

7. Ibid., 199.

8. Ibid., 30.

9. Ibid., 30.

10. Ibid., 311.

11. Ibid., 238-239.

12. Ibid., 241.

13. Ibid., 307.

14. Karel Van Wolferen, *The Enigma of Japanese Power*, 125.

15. Ibid., 125.

16. Carl C. Landegger, "Increase in Global Competition Demands Development of U.S. Industrial Policy," *Pulp and Paper*, August 1993, 91.

17. Robert Reich, *The Next American Frontier*, 178.

18. Ibid., 178.

19. Ibid., 234.

20. Ibid., 235.

21. Louis Galambos and Joseph Pratt, *The Rise of the Corporate Commonwealth*, 140.

22. Robert Reich, *The Work of Nations*, 254.

23. *Traffic Management*, July 1990, 27.

24. Daniel F. Burton Jr., "High-Tech Competitiveness," 123.

25. Louis Galambos and Joseph Pratt, *The Rise of the Corporate Commonwealth*, 141.

26. Ibid., 141-142

27. "An interview with Ex-DARPA Director Craig Fields," *Technology Review*, Feburary/March 1991, 35.

28. Ibid., 38.

29. Ibid., 37.

30. Ibid., 36.

31. "Uncle Sams Helping Hand," *The Economist*, April 2, 1994, 77.

32. William J. Spencer and Peter Grindley, "SEMATECH After Five Years: High Technology Consortia and U.S. Competitiveness," *California Management Review*, Summer 1993, 14.

33. U.S. Technology Strategy Emerges," *Science*, April 5, 1991, 23.

34. "Evoloution of Federal Involvment," *Congressional Digest*, December 1992, 291.

35. William Spencer and Petcr Grindley, "SEMATECH After Five Years: High Technology Consortia and U.S. Competitiveness," Summer 1993, 10.

36. "U.S. Technology Strategy Emerges," *Science*, April 5 1994, 23.

37. "Is Sematech A Model for Global Competitiveness," *R & D Magazine*, October 25, 1993, 28.

38. William J Spencer and Peter Grindley, "SEMATECH After Five Years: High Technology Consortia and U.S. Competitiveness," Summer 1993, 18.

39. William M Evan and Paul Olk, "R&D Consortia: A New U.S. Organizational Form," *Loan Management Review*, Spring 1990, 39.

40. Ibid., 39.

41. "Evolution of Federal Involvement, Congressional Digest, December 1992, 291.

42. Ibid., 291.

43. Ibid., 291.

44. Frank Swoboda, "Putting U.S. Manufacturers to the Test," *The Washington Post National Weekly Edition*, May 30-June 5, 1994, 23.

45. Ibid., 23.

46. Robert Reich, "Metamorphosis of the American Worker," *Business Month*, November 1990, 59.

47. Robert Reich, *The Work of Nations*, 226.

48. Peter Drucker, *The New Realites*, 234.

49. Robert Reich, *The Work of Nations*, 227.

50. Peter Drucker, *The New Realities*, 234-235.

51. Robert Reich, *The Work of Nations*, 228.

52. "Competing World Economies," *Congressional Digest*, December 1992, 293.

53. "Manufacturers Offer Modernization Plan," *Industrial Distribution*, April 1991, 11.

54. Kurt Woolley, "Economic Expansion in the United States; Beyond Free Market Manufacturing," *IM*, May/June 1990, 8.

55. "Evolution of Federal Involvement," Congressional Digest, December 1992, 291.

56. "NIST: Measuring up to a New Task," *Science*, March 26, 1993, 1818.

57. "Is There, Then a Role for Government in High Tech? ," *Forbes*, May 10, 1993, 26.

58. Bennett Harrison, "The Real Council of Competitiveness," *Technology Review*, July 1992, 65.

59. Brink Lindsey, "SEMATECH: The Wrong Solution," *The Journal of Commerce*, January 17, 1992, 7.

60. Robert Kuttner, "Facing up to Industrial Policy," 42.

61. "Competing World Economies," *Congressional Digest*, December 1992, 293.

62. Ibid., 293.

Epilogue

Statistical data for this book was collected for the years 1981-1992, a period of awakening for U.S. industries. During subsequent years, the pace of change has been at least as dynamic and worth some comment as to the direction that companies are being pushed resulting from the rapid momentum created by the Information Age.

Less than fifty years ago school children were drilled to scramble under their desks as protection from the A-bomb in case of an attack by the Russian enemies. That generation (generally know as the 'baby boomers') has rarely known a time in their lives free from an acute awareness of a bipolar world in which the communists were a threatening force. As a result, top priority was given by the U.S. government during most of these fifty years to the establishment of a massive and powerful military complex in order to assure a strong defense against the communist menace.

In the years following the World War II there was a strong sense of confidence in the success of the United States, not only as a democracy, but also as an economic power beyond competition from any other country. Our wealth was determined by tangible items, and as leaders in the industrial revolution, we had not only the economies of scale to produce it, but also a large national market to consume it. Our country was in the forefront of all that was *big*—big machines, big labor unions, big hospitals, big factories, big universities, and of course, the classic big cars. As a country rich in natural resources, we were able to easily, and perhaps most importantly, cheaply, support all this *bigness*.

Confidence in the U.S. economy and way of life was so firmly established that initially the business community did not understand the implications of the Information Age as it moved in to take the place of the Industrial Age. In the 1970's, the era of *bigness* and *tangibility* had begun to change. Rather than the Industrial Age, we were entering something far less tangible—the Age of Information. As a sign of the times, in 1971 the U.S. went off the gold standard and the country's capital was no longer determined by the backup tangibility of gold, but rather by the judgments of world financial markets. Up to this time a company's worth was generally based on its economies of scale—its tangible assets—but that was no longer compatible with the products and services of the Information Age.

The established political and business leaders at the dawn of the Information Age (1970s) clung tightly to old patterns and resisted attempts to establish new paradigms. The United States had become a great power based on a large military complex, economies of scale, and a top-heavy managerial organization. As these leaders saw it, new paradigms were threatening and potentially destructive, particularly in relation to their own power and influence. The prevailing paradigm had worked wonders in the Industrial Age, but the lethargy and drag it created at the beginning of the Information Age, began to undermine the country's economic base.

By the mid-1980s, predictions for the U.S.'s decline were very real, with writers such as Paul Kennedy in his *The Rise and Fall of the Great Powers* noting that ". . . a very heavy investment in armaments, while bringing greater security in the short term, may so erode the commercial competitiveness of the American economy that the nation will be less secure in the long term."[1] At the time he wrote the book, which was published in 1987, Kennedy's assumptions were probably quite correct because defense spending under President Reagan had reached one of its highest peaks, and the economy was reeling under the burden of a growing budget deficit and trade deficits, particularly with Japan. Kennedy believed that the trends of the past two decades (1965-1985) would continue on indefinitely, and therefore insure the fulfillment of his prophecy of a profound shift in the world's productive balance.[2]

What Kennedy's prophecy did not include was that within two years of his book's publication the breakdown of the Soviet Union would ensue. The world which had, up to then, been a world of two powerful polarities, was left with only one superpower, the United States. That changed everything. Now, rather than an *us* against *them* posture, for the first time in the *boomers* lives they are looking at a world which is bound together in a global capitalist system.[3] The emphasis is no longer on who has the greatest military complex, but rather which society has the greatest capability to conquer the world economically.

In 1990, an official report released in the aftermath of the G7 summit stated, "American manufacturing has never been in more trouble than it is now."[4] Just seven years ago the nation's mood was one of gloom regarding Japan's trade superiority and our own inability to compete. This year's [1997] Summit of Eight has had quite a different story as "America is now in the seventh year of an orderly expansion growing at an annual average rate of 2.5%, with no significant downturn in sight. Unemployment stands at around 4.8%; yet, astonishingly, there are no signs of inflation. The stock market is at an all-time high; Americans are being paid more, and they expect to hand their prosperity on to their children. That old ghost worker, insecurity, seems to have drifted away. To the perplexity and envy of the Denver summiteers, America, with over 12m new jobs since 1991, now seems to be an unstoppable job-creating machine."[5] All the analysts are trying to figure it out: What have we done right, and what are we about to do wrong? There is always that underlying assumption that we are just waiting for the 'other shoe to fall'.

Of course, on the one hand, there is no way to know what surprises are ahead for us, just as Paul Kennedy in *The Rise and Fall of the Great Powers* could not have predicted the demise of the Soviet Union and the shifts of power throughout Eastern Europe. On the other hand, we no longer can make judgments based on the Industrial Age experience. During my undergraduate years I had a statistics professor who, on the first day of class, had us all stand on our chairs, suggesting that from this new position we would perceive the room differently. He explained that in the study of statistics we should also start to see very ordinary events from a different perspective. In this sense, I have tried to connect the Information Age, as it manifests itself, to a new paradigm rather than to hold firm to the *truths* as studied in relation to the Industrial Age.

Whereas the economy of the Industrial Age was based on *tangible* items—big machines, factories, labor unions, and so forth, the Information Age is based on the *intangible*. A company's wealth is no longer a matter of who has the most physical assets but rather on how its potential for success is perceived by the stockholders. *Big* is no longer the desired outcome; the emphasis is now on efficiency, quality, and price and when appropriate, on speed and the powerful technology that drives it.

One of the most significant results of the Information Age has been the globalization of the U.S. economy, not only from the point of view of businesses, but also from the point of view of the consumers who look to the U.S. to fulfill their needs for consumer goods. Becoming competitive in the global economy has not been an easy road for U.S. businesses, particularly the large, well-established ones.

The first step for many companies was to eat 'humble pie' and acknowledge that the old patterns with top-heavy management, large, inefficient work forces, and uncompetitively-priced goods were no longer sufficient, or

even appropriate. They had to look to their strongest competitor, Japan, as a model for success in the global market. Based on lessons from Japan, many companies moved to change their management styles by empowering their employees, organizing teamwork, and encouraging creativity and innovation. Often the results were phenomenal, with increases in productivity, quality, and efficiency that would have been unheard of under the previous methods.

Beyond that, though, was the realization that Americans had a cultural advantage over the Japanese as it relates to the business community. No society in the world is quite so open and individualistic as the American society. Whereas the Japanese emphasize the importance of the community and creative thinking is squelched, the Americans make individualists and creative thinkers their heros. An article in the June 9, 1997 *U.S. News & World Report* states that in spite of "leading international scores in math and science, Japan has produced a grand total of just five Nobel science and medicine laureates—versus America's 191."[6] There is more than one reason for this paucity of representation by the Japanese, but certainly one of the reasons is the negativity associated in that culture with individualistic thinking. Another *U.S. News and World Report* article points out that the Japanese have not been able to compete with the Americans in the software market because "The prowess of American programmers is partly the triumph of a cowboy type of approach to software development, in which an inspired individual, or small group of programmers, produces a program faster than a 1,000-person army, as is the case in a Japanese software 'factory'. Microsoft, for one, organizes its programmers into the smallest possible cells, in order to avoid a 'factory' feel."[7]

There is no doubt that predictions of economic decline have been reversed as a result of American flexibility and willingness to institute new management practices while emphasizing the tradition of individualism. We are still at the very beginning of this Information Age and change is so rapid, one can hardly imagine the innovations and their impacts even ten years down the road. There are, of course, many prophets of doom, and potentially, any number of external factors could negatively impact the economic prosperity we are experiencing in the latter part of the 1990s. Nevertheless, any analysis of the economy and the potential for U.S. competitiveness in the global economy should be based on a new paradigm as it relates specifically to the Information Age and not tied to the usual business cycle expectations of the Industrial Age.

NOTES

1. Kennedy, Paul., *The Rise and Fall of the Great Powers:* New York: Random House, 1964, 532.

2. Ibid., 538.

3. Sachs, Jeffrey. "The Limits of Convergence." *The Economist*, June 14, 1997, 19.

4. "Back to Glory Days." *The Economist*, June 21, 1997, 27.

5. "Bill Clinton's Golden Moment," *The Economist,* 21 June, 1997, 16.

6. "Labs' Labor Lost in Japan, " *U.S. News & World Report,* June 9, 1997, 42.

7. "In Software, It's Still Bambi vs. Godzilla," *U.S. News & World Report,* June 2, 1997, 49.

Bibliography

Alster, Norm. "In Fighting Trim." *Forbes 10* (June 1991): 51.

Altany, David. "The Race With No Finish Line." *Industry Week* (Jan. 8, 1990): 105.

Aviel, David. "Why the United States Isn't Winning the Trade War with Japan." *IM* (Mar./April 1990): 14.

Barrier, Michael. "When 'Just in Time' Just Isn't Enough." *Nations Business* (Nov. 1992): 30.

Berger, Warren. "The McLaughlin Legacy Condensing the Digest." *Fozio* (Feb. 1991): 44.

Bergsten, Fred. *International Adjustment and Financing.* Washington D.C. Institute for International Economics, 1991.

Bergsten, Fred. "The World Economy After the Cold War." *California Management Review* (Winter 1992): 53.

Bergstrom, Robin P. "Maybe you Simply Need to Change Lanes." *Production* (February 1992): 48.

Berss, Marcia. "Under Control" *Forbes* (Jan. 31, 1994): 32.

Blecker, Robert. *Beyond the Twin Deficits.* Armonk, NY: M.E Sharpe, 1992.

"A Blueprint to ISO 9000." *Machine Design 22* (Oct. 1993): 226.

Bolwijn, P.T. and T. Kumpe. "Manufacturing in the 1990's Productivity, Flexibility and Innovation." *Long Range Planning* (Aug. 1990): 46.

Bonker, Don. *Americans Trade Crises.* Boston: Houghton Mifflin Company, 1988.

Buckley, Peter, C.L. Pass and Kate Prescott. "Foreign Market Servicing Strategies and Competitiveness." *Journal of General Management* (Winter 1991): 34.

Buiday, Robert. "Re-engineering One Firms Product Development and Anothers Service Delivery." *Planning Review* (Mar./Apr. 1993): 16.

Burton, Daniel F. "High Technology Competitiveness." *Foreign Policy* (Fall 1993): 118.

Carlson, Paul F. "The Long and Short of Strategic Planning." *The Journal of Business Strategy* (May/June 1990): 18-16.

"Competing World Economies." *Congressional Digest* (Dec. 1992): 295.

Congress House, Task Force on Economic Policy of the Committee on the Budget, *International Trade and the Federal Deficit*, 19 Oct. 1985 Washington D.C. GPO.

Congress, Joint Economic Committee. Subcommittee on Economic Goals and Intergovernmental Policy, *Impact on the Dollar on U.S. Competitiveness*, Mar. 12, 1985. Washington D.C. GPO.

Congress Senate Committee on Finance. Subcommittee on Deficit, Debt Management and International Debt. *Long-term Impact of the Federal Deficit on the US Economy*. June 5, 1992. Washington DC: GPO.

Congress Subcommittee on Economic Goals and Intergovernmental Policy of the Joint Economic Committee, *Economic Effects of Trade Legislation*. Sept. 18, 1985. Washington DC. GPO.

"Corporate R&D." *FW* (Oct. 1, 1991): 32

"Delivery Under Pressure." *Automotive Industries* (Dec. l993): 63.

Deming, Edwards W. *Quality, Productivity and Competitive Position*. Cambridge, MA: MIT Center for Advanced Engineering Study, 1982.

Drucker, Peter. *The New Realities*. New York: Harper and Row, 1989.

Economic Report of the President 1993. Washington D.C.: GPO, 1993.466, Table B-103.

Economic Report of the President 1994. Washington D.C. GPO, 1994.

Evan, William M and Paul Olk. "R&D Consortia: A New U.S. Organizational Form." *Loan Management Review* (Spring 1990): 39.

"Evolution of Federal Involvement." *Congressional Digest* (Dec. 1992):291.

Galambos, Louis and Joseph Pratt. *The Rise of the Corporate Commonwealth*. New York: Basic Books, 1989.

Getterman, Ken. "No Change, but Relentless Change." *Modern Machine Shop* (Mar. 1991): 94.

Goldhar, Joel D. and David Lei. "The Shape of Twenty-First Century Global Manufacturing." *The Journal of Business Strategy* (Mar./Apr. 1991): 58.

Hamel, David. "DMF Easy If You Know How." *Machine Design* (Jan. 8, 1993): 27. 242.

Hamel, Gary and C.K. Prahalad. "Strategic Intent." *Harvard Business Review* (March/April 1986): 117.

Hamel, Gary and C.K. Prahalad. "Megamarketing." *Harvard Business Review* (May/June 1988): 17.

Harrison, Bennett. "The Real Council of Competitiveness," *Technology Review* (July 1992): 65.

"Incorporating a Creative Culture." *International Management* (May 1990): 82.

"An interview with Ex-DARPA Director Craig Fields." *Technology Review* (Feb./Mar. 1991): 35.

"Is There, Then a Role for Government in High Tech?" *Forbes* (May 10, 1993): 26.

"Is Sematech A Model for Global Competitiveness." *R & D Magazine* (Oct. 25, 1993): 28.

Jacobs, Michael T. *Short Term America*. Boston MA: Harvard Business School Press, 1991, 5.

"Japan: Should We Copy to Compete?" *Automation*, 61.

Johnson, Wayne. "Carrier Says Cutback will Help it Compete." *Air Conditioning Heating and Refrigeration News* (July 27, 1993): 3.

Johnson, Wayne. "Carrier Team Outcomes Furnace Lines with New Products in Only Twenty Months." *Air Conditioning, Heating and Refrigeration News* (July 12, 1993): 6.

Kennedy, Paul. *The Rise and Fall of the Great Powers*. New York: Vintage Books, 1987.

Kharbanda, O.P. "Japan's Lessons for the West." *CMA Magazine* (Feb. 1992): 243.

Kosaku, Yoshlda. "Deming's Management Philosophy: Does It Work in the U.S. as well as in Japan." *The Columbia Journal of World Business* (Fall 1989): 10-17.

Kotler, Phillip. "Megamarketing." *Harvard Business Review* (Mar./Apr. 1986): 1 17.

Krugman, Paul. "Competitiveness Does It Matter?" *Fortune* (Mar. 7, 1994): 1 10.

Krugman, Paul. "Myths and Realities of U.S. Competitiveness." *Science* (Nov. 8, 1991): 109.

Krugman, Paul. *The Age of Diminished Expectations*. Cambridge, MA: The MIT Press, 1991.

Kuttner, Robert. "Facing up to Industrial Policy." *New York Times Magazine* (Apr. 19, 1992): 26.

Landegger, Carl C. "Increase in Global Competition Demands Development of U.S. Industrial Policy." *Pulp and Paper* (August 1993): 91.

Leavic, Bill. "HR Executive Takes A Direct Approach." *HR Magazine* (February 1990): 51.

Lee, Mushin. "Samsung uses Theory 2 to Become A Living Organization." *IM* (September/October 1992): 30.

Lenz, Allen J. *Narrowing the U.S. Current Account Deficit.* Washington D.C.: Institute for International Economics, 1992.

Leontiades, Milton. " The Japanese Art of Managing Diversity." *The Journal of Business Strategy* (March/April 1991): 30.

Levitt, Theodore. "The Globalization of Markets." *Harvard Business Review* (May/June 1983): 92.

Lindert, Peter. *International Economics. 9th Ed.* Boston: Irwin, 1991.

Lindsey, Brink. "Sematech: The Wrong Solution." *The Journal of Commerce* (January 17, 1992): 7.

Lodge, George C. *The American Disease.* New York: Alfred A Knopf, 1984.

Maital, Shlomo. "Future Winners." *Across the Board* (December 1991): 7.

Malambre, Alfred Jr. *Within our Means.* New York: Random House, 1991.

"Manufactures Offer Modernization Plan." *Industrial Distribution* (April 1991): 11.

McGlennhen, John S. "Can you Manage in the New Economy." *Industry Week* (October 21, 1991): 27.

Mckenna, Joseph F. "Newport News Shipbuilding, Builds More than Ships." *Industry Week* (November 1, 1993): 39.

Mckenna, Joseph. "From JIT With Love." *Industry Week* (August 17, 1992): 45.

Mckenna, Joseph. "SPQ." *Industry Week* (October 21, 1991): 49.

Milliot, Jim. "Readers Digest Focusing on Cost Containment in 1994." *Publishers Weekly* (November 15, 1993): 22.

Mtari, Michael. "High Tech Makes for High Touch." *Industry Week* (August 17, 1992): 45.

Munchus, G III. "Employer-Employee Based Quality Circles in Japan: Human Resource Policy Implications for American Firms." *Academy of Management Review* (1983): 255-261.

Musselwhite, Christopher W. "Time Based Innovation: The New Competitive Advantage." *Training and Development Journal* (January 1990): 54-55.

Najar, Sylvia. "The American Economy, Back on Top." *The New York Times* (February 27, 1994): Section 3, 6.

"National Industrial Policy." *Congressional Digest* (December 1992): 298.

"NIST. Measuring Up To A New Task." *Science* (March 26, 1993): 1818.

Nowlin, William. "Restructuring In Manufacturing Management, Work and Labor Relations." *IM* (November/December 1990): 7.

Paloncy, Steven. "Team Approach Cuts Costs." *HR Magazine* (November 1990): 61.

Parring, Robert. "U.S. Trade Deficit and International Competition." *Business Economics* (January 1994): 22.

Perry, Toni. "Staying with the Basics." *HR Magazine* (November 1990): 73.

Porter, Michael. "The Competitive Advantage of Nations" *Harvard Business Review* (March-April 1990): 84-85.

Prahalad, C.K. and Gary Hamel. "The Core Competence of the Corporation." *Harvard Business Review* (May/June 1990): 79.

Reich, Robert. *The Next American Frontier*. New York: Times Books, 1983.

Reich, Robert. *The Work of Nations*. New York: Alfred A Knopf, 1991.

Reich, Robert. "Who Is Us?" *Harvard Business Review* (January-February 1990): 59.

Ropper, Norman. "Reinventing the Factory with Lifelong Learning." *Training* (March 1993): 55.

Salk, George Jr. "Time—The Next Source of Competitive Advantage." *Harvard Business Review* (July/August 1988): 41.

Scally, John. "Actions Speak Louder then Buzzwords." *National Productivity Review* (Autumn 1993): 453-456.

Scott, Bruce R. and George C. Lodge *U.S. Competitiveness in the World Economy*. Boston: Harvard Business School Press, 1985.

Sheehan, Christopher. "Two Avenues of Growth for the Paper Industry." *The Office* (November 1991): 56.

Sheldon, Robert. and Brian Kleiner. "What Japanese Management Techniques can (or Should) be Applied by American Managers." *IM* (May/June 1990): 19.

Simon, Herman. "Lessons from Germany's Miosre Giants." *Harvard Business Review* (March/April 1992): 116.

Smothers, Norman P. "Patterns of Japanese Strategy; Strategic Combination of Strategies." *Strategic Management Journal* (April 1990): 521.

Spencer, William J. and Peter Grindley. "Sematech After Five Years: High Technology Consortia and U.S. Competitiveness." *California Management Review* (Summer 1993): 17.

Swoboda, Frank. "Putting U.S. Manufactures to the Test." *The Washington Post National Weekly Edition* (May 30, June 5, 1994): 23.

Tatom, John. "Is An Infrastructure Crises Lowering the Nation's Productivity." *Review* (November/December 1993): 4.

Taylor, Charles R. "Prospering in the 90's" *Across the Board* (January/February 1992): 44.

"Turning A New Leaf In Recycling of Office Waste Paper." *The Office* (November 1991): 56.

"Uncle Sams Helping Hand" *The Economist* (April 2, 1994): 77.

U.S. Department of Commerce International Trade Administration. "An Assessment of U.S. Competitiveness in High Technology Industries." (GPO 1983).

U.S. Department of Commerce International Trade Administration. "Improving U.S. Competitiveness." (GPO 1987): 19.

"U.S. Technology Strategy Emerges." *Science* (April 5, 1994): 23.

Verespy, Michael. "World Class Organizations." *Industry Week* (January 16, 1990): 22.

Vogel, David. *Fluctuating Fortunes.* New York: Basic Books Inc., 1989.

Weidenbaum, Murray. "Filling in the Hollowed-Out Corporation: The Competitive Status of U.S. Manufacturing." *Business Economics* (January 1990): 20.

Weyr, Thomas. "The Wiring of Simon and Schuster." *Publishers Weekly* (June 1, 1992): 33.

Wolferen, Karel Van. *the Enigma of Japanese Power.* New York: Random House, 1989.

Woolley, Kurt. "Economic Expansion in the United States; Beyond Free Marketing Manufacturing," *IM* (May/June 1990): 8.

Index